Food, family & friends

Quick & Easy Recipes for Everyday Occasions

Food, Family & Friends was produced
by Time-Life Custom Publishing especially for The Pampered Chef

The Pampered Chef, Ltd.

President
Doris K. Christopher

Executive Vice President
Jay W. Christopher

Vice President of Sales & Services
Janis M. Gilmore

Manager of Product Development
Amy Raczka

Manager of Communications
Julie Bruser

With special thanks to the thousands of Pampered Chef Consultants and customers who made this book possible.

Questions related to Pampered Chef products should be directed to your local Pampered Chef Consultant, or to Pampered Chef Customer Service:

1–708–261–8850

The Pampered Chef, Ltd.
350 S. Route 53
Addison, IL 60101

Time Life, Inc.

President and CEO
John M. Fahey

President, Time-Life Books
John Hall

Time-Life Custom Publishing

Vice President and Publisher
Terry Newell

Director of Custom Publishing
Frances C. Mangan

Manager, Sales and Operations
Phyllis Gardner

Manager, New Business Development
Rebecca C. Wheeler

Associate Program Manager
Wendy Blythe

Editorial Director
Donia Ann Steele

Project Editor
Jennifer Pearce

Senior Art Director
Christopher M. Register

Design
David Fridberg

Food Editor
Lisa Cherkasky

Photography
Reneé Comet

Production Managers
Carolyn Bounds
Marlene Zack

Quality Assurance Manager
Miriam Newton

Special Contributors
Jody Boozel
Esther Del Rosario
Cynthia McMahon
Jenny Rugland

Contents

Spiced Apple Stir-Fry
Cranberry-Apple Crisp
(see page 68)

Grilled Chicken & Vegetable Kebabs
Shrimp Deviled Eggs
(see page 56)

$\mathcal{I}$ntroduction

15TH ANNIVERSARY YEAR

In honor of The Pampered Chef's fifteenth anniversary and its mission to enhance the quality of family life, we are pleased to present this collection of recipes celebrating "food, family and friends." With these recipes, you will be able to turn any occasion into a fun and memorable gathering.

Foods prepared with love provide family and friends with common memories — of tastes, smells, laughter and shared efforts in the kitchen. And of special meals together. So, whether you want to commemorate a birthday or holiday or acknowledge a good report card, you will find quick, easy and delicious menus in these pages to help make the meal a success. You may even find yourself creating some new family traditions!

We hope you like these *Food, Family & Friends* recipes and that you will share them with loved ones for many years to come. Enjoy!

Chicken Cacciatore (see page 78)

The Pampered Chef began with one woman's vision during the "me generation" decade of the 1980s to refocus our attention on what matters most — sharing quality time with our families. Guided by that vision and by a strong entrepreneurial spirit, Doris Christopher launched a new business that eventually grew into The Pampered Chef. It had a remarkably simple premise: to provide quality kitchen tools that would make food preparation easier and thus encourage families to have meals together regularly.

Doris Christopher in her 1980 Chicago home with some early Pampered Chef products

Before founding The Pampered Chef, Doris had worked as a home economist and educator, frequently using and demonstrating high-quality kitchen tools and equipment. To her frustration, she had discovered that the kitchen tools sold in local stores were not of the quality available to her as a professional. All too often, the products were poorly designed, the salespeople ill-informed and the consumer product information inadequate, if it existed at all.

Doris saw the need for quality kitchen products that offered consumers complete information about their use and care. She also recognized that the home presented a natural setting for selling these products. Customers could see how the products worked, try them on the spot and even test the results with actual recipes prepared during in-home demonstrations. This comfortable, low-key, show-and-tell sales approach, she reasoned, would not only appeal to people's natural curiosity about the products, but would also serve to develop a high level of customer trust and satisfaction in them. And, indeed, she was right: Today, The Pampered Chef enjoys the loyalty of millions of customers nationwide.

The home demonstration method of selling also provided Doris with a flexible work schedule, enabling her to maintain a balance between her career and family responsibilities as she got her business off the ground. Helping people hold on to quality time with their families was, after all, at the heart of her vision for The Pampered Chef. Soon, as the company began to grow, Doris was able to offer others the opportunity for meaningful and flexible part-time employment — the kind of employment that could accommodate the demands of modern family life. Today, The Pampered Chef employs almost 20,000 Kitchen Consultants, or sales representatives, across the country. Each is an independent businessperson who sets his or her own hours and is therefore able to work around the schedule demands of children and family and even, in some cases, other, full-time employment.

1980 home of Doris and Jay Christopher, and original head-quarters for Doris' fledgling business

BEGINNINGS: 1980 - 1989

The Pampered Chef began humbly fifteen years ago in the basement of a two-story house in the Chicago suburb of River Forest. It started with an investment of $3,000 and a sales force of one — Doris Christopher. Doris's husband, Jay, helped with all aspects of the business, stocking inventory and filling and sending out customer orders from a simple price list as well as business mentoring and coaching. Doris, an educator by training, had no prior business experience before starting the company. During its first three months, The Pampered Chef achieved $10,000 in sales. By the end of the first year, sales had increased to more than $50,000 and the sales force had grown to twelve.

One of the thousands of Kitchen Shows held by The Pampered Chef's Kitchen Consultants in the past year

An energetic young family, as well as a new company, was flourishing and growing in that suburban Chicago home. Doris and Jay had two young daughters. Yet because her working hours were flexible, Doris found that she was able to spend quality time with her children while running a fledgling company.

The Pampered Chef grew at an astounding rate. In 1983, sales climbed to more than $200,000, and then more than doubled the following year, forcing the company to move out of Doris and Jay's basement and into a 2,500-square foot facility. By the end of 1986, the number of Kitchen Consultants had increased to 200 and the company printed its first photographic product catalog. Another important milestone of that year was the company's membership in the Direct Selling Association, which affiliated The Pampered Chef with the giants in the direct sales industry.

On January 1, 1987, Jay officially joined the company as vice-president of operations. The Pampered Chef had grown enough to require full-time management of product ordering, warehousing and distribution. Meanwhile, Doris focused her efforts on working with the growing number of Kitchen Consultants — some 700 by the end of 1989.

TREMENDOUS GROWTH: 1990 - PRESENT

In 1990, The Pampered Chef was featured in articles appearing in two popular magazines, *Woman's Day* and *U.S.News & World Report*, which generated a great deal of publicity and enthusiasm

The Pampered Chef's headquarters in Addison, Illinois

about the company. Thousands of new Kitchen Consultants joined the sales force as a result of this and later media exposure, and by the end of 1992, the company had active Consultants in all fifty states.

By then, The Pampered Chef was recognized as a new leader in the direct selling industry. In June 1991, Doris was elected to a term on the Direct Selling Association Board of Directors. Early in 1993, the company was showcased as the "Company in Focus" at the Direct Selling Association's Regional Developmental Conference. During the following year, a special annual edition of *Inc.* magazine ranked The Pampered Chef 131st among the 500 fastest-growing privately held companies in America.

A Socially Responsible Company

*A*s a business leader in a food-related industry, The Pampered Chef sought to use its position to make others aware of the need to help the hungry in America. So, in 1991, Doris initiated the Round-Up From The Heart program, a company-wide commitment to promoting good nutrition and sharing resources in order to help solve the growing hunger crisis in America.

This unique program is a partnership effort between The Pampered Chef's Kitchen Consultants, customers and corporate employees and Second Harvest, a Chicago-based, nonprofit organization whose mission is to feed the hungry by soliciting and distributing surplus food to a nationwide network of charitable food banks.

Each year The Pampered Chef donates one dollar for each Kitchen Show that its Kitchen Consultants

hold between September 1 and December 31. These funds go directly to Second Harvest. Customers of The Pampered Chef participate in the fund-raising program by "rounding up" their order total to the nearest dollar. These funds are sent to Second Harvest food banks in the region where the donations originate, making this a national program with local impact.

The phenomenal growth of The Pampered Chef has shown no signs of slowing down. In June 1994, the company moved to its current 223,000-square-foot headquarters in Addison, Illinois. The building includes generous warehouse space, ample parking and a totally refurbished interior to accommodate a growing staff of more than 400 people. The company has also installed a computerized packing and distribution system to increase the speed and accuracy of orders.

Holidays are a time for special family gatherings in the Christopher home

This year marks The Pampered Chef's fifteenth anniversary celebration. The entrepreneurial vision that was born in a suburban Chicago basement in 1980 has grown under Doris Christopher's leadership into a significant multimillion dollar company. Yet despite its size, The Pampered Chef remains true to its original vision: providing quality products that enhance family life.

Corporate employees of the Pampered Chef participate in food drives and fund-raising product sales, and volunteer time as packers for local food banks. Administrative costs of the Round-Up From The Heart program are also donated by The Pampered Chef.

During the first year of the program, $70,000 was raised, far exceeding expectations. The amount has increased each year since, with a total of $378,000 raised in 1994. In all, during the first four years of the campaign, The Pampered Chef has donated more than three-quarters of a million dollars to Second Harvest food banks throughout the United States. This success underscores The Pampered Chef's resolve to provide its ever-growing family of Consultants and employees with an opportunity to work together to make a difference.

For its successful Round-Up From The Heart program, The Pampered Chef was honored with the 1993 "Vision For Tomorrow Award" from the Direct Selling Association. Second Harvest also presented the company with the "Second Harvest Sponsorship Award" at the organization's 1993 national convention.

Equipment

1. Stoneware Baking Bowl
2. Bread Baking Crock
3. Dough and Pizza Roller
4. 15-inch Round Baking Stone
5. 15-inch Oven-to-Table Rack
6. 13-inch Round Baking Stone
7. 13-inch and Rectangle Oven-to-Table Rack
8. Pizza Cutter
9. 9" x 13" Baker
10. 12" x 15" Rectangle Baking Stone
11. Oven Mitt
12. Bamboo Spatula
13. Stir-Fry Skillet
14. Deep Dish Baker
15. Stoneware Loaf Pan
16. Mini Baking Bowl
17. 8-inch Mini Baker

Equipment

1. Wondercup 2-cup
2. Batter Bowl with Lid
3. Pocket Thermometer
4. Lemon Aid
5. 8-inch Open Sauté Pan
6. 11-inch Square Griddle

Generation II
10-piece Cookware Set:

7a. 1½-quart saucepan with lid
7b. 2-quart saucepan with lid
7c. 4-quart casserole with lid
7d. 10-inch frying pan
7e. 6-quart Dutch oven with lid
7f. stainless steel steamer

8. Apple Corer
9. Apple Wedger
10. Apple Peeler/Corer/Slicer
11. 10-inch Whisk
12. Stainless Steel Scoops -
    medium and small
13. Garlic Press
14. Zyliss Food Chopper
15. Mini-Serving Spatula
16. Ice Cream Dipper
17. Non-Stick Bear/Rabbit
    Pancake Mold
18. Pumpkin Cutter

Equipment

1. 8" x 6" Bar Board
2. 13" x 9" Cutting Board
3. Grooved 18" x 12" Cutting Board
4. 5-inch Self-Sharpening Utility Knife
5. Vegetable Peeler
6. Garnisher
7. Tullen Kitchen Cutters
8. 3-inch Self-Sharpening Paring Knife
9. Lemon Zester/Scorer
10. V-Shaped Cutter
11. Leifheit Two-Way Egg Slicer
12. 3-inch Cut-N-Seal
13. 4-inch Cut-N-Seal
14. Quikut Paring Knife
15. Serrated Bread Knife
16. Kitchen Parchment
17. Springform Pan Set
18. Valtrompia Bread Tubes
19. Non-Stick Cooling Rack
20. Mini-Tart Shaper
21. Mini-Muffin Pan
22. Super Scraper
23. Skinny Scraper
24. Bamboo Spoon Set
25. Flan Pan Set
26. Cake Tester
27. Stoneware Gingerbread House Mold
28. Leifheit Decorating Set
29. Zyliss Cheese Grater

PAPER MAID

kitchen parchment

THE NO-STICK PAN LINER
THAT COMES OFF IN A ROLL

Good Food, Good Fun for All Seasons

One of the greatest rewards about my work with The Pampered Chef is sharing with friends all over the country some of my family's ideas on how to have fun with food preparation and presentation. Hash browns, eggs and cheese, for instance, turned into a "pizza," make a breakfast a special occasion. Or cupcakes made to look like ice cream cones or a yellow cake dressed up like a football turn ho-hum desserts into something memorable.

Doris Christopher at home with daughters Julie and Kelley, and husband Jay

In the recipe sections that follow, we show you many such ways to enjoy the occasions that each new season of the year brings. The book begins here with a festive spread for January 1st, the day devoted to bright new beginnings. Winter occasions are followed in turn by ideas for spring, summer and fall, winding up with the Christmas holidays. Scattered throughout the book are "anytime" events that don't depend on any particular season, just your family's imagination and sense of fun.

Best of all, The Pampered Chef tools and equipment that are featured help to make the preparations quick and easy, so the chef can have as much fun as the rest of the family!

Enjoy!

Doris Christopher

Doris Christopher

New Year's Brunch

It's the beginning of a new year, and the whole world, it seems, is making resolutions. Why not make yours a promise to spend more time with family and friends, enjoying conversation, laughter, and of course, good food. Get off on the right foot by inviting the gang over for a casual New Year's Brunch. Once the coffee's poured, have some fun recalling the year gone by, and foretelling what lies ahead. Where will YOU be a year from now? If you keep your resolution, chances are you'll be right back here, sharing another brunch and figuring out how many of the group's predictions came true.

BOUNTIFUL BRUNCH
PIZZA

∎

RASPBERRY-CHEESE
COFFEE CAKE

∎

PEELED, SLICED
ORANGES AND
GRAPEFRUIT

∎

CHAMPAGNE

∎

COFFEE

Crust:

1 package (24 ounces) frozen
  shredded hash brown patties,
  thawed, and broken apart

1 egg, beaten

Salt and ground black pepper to
  taste

Egg & Cheddar Topping:

7 eggs

½ cup milk

1 ½ cups shredded Cheddar
  cheese

Salt and ground black pepper to
  taste

Optional Toppings:

Chopped onions

Chopped green peppers

Sliced mushrooms

Chopped ham

Bacon, cooked and crumbled

BOUNTIFUL BRUNCH PIZZA

Prepare crust: Preheat oven to 400° F. Cover 15-inch Round
Baking Stone with Kitchen Parchment Paper. Combine potatoes
with beaten egg in a large bowl, then spread over parchment-
covered Baking Stone to form 14-inch circle, pressing firmly with
back of spoon. Sprinkle with salt and pepper. Bake 20 minutes.

Prepare egg and cheddar topping: Meanwhile, whisk eggs and
milk in Batter Bowl; microwave, uncovered, at 100 percent power
for 3 minutes. Stir well. Microwave at 100 percent power 3 minutes longer. Stir well. Spread cooked eggs evenly over baked potato crust. Top with your choice of optional ingredients, sprinkle
with seasonings and Cheddar cheese and bake 10 minutes longer.
Slide Breakfast Pizza off parchment paper onto serving platter. Cut
into wedges with Pizza Cutter and serve hot.

Yield: 10 to 12 servings

Using the Egg Slicer

*Use Egg Slicer to cut hard-boiled eggs,
farm-fresh mushrooms and other small
foods into thin, even slices. To create a
strawberry fan, place berry in Slicer and
cut nearly all the way through, leaving
top intact.*

Crust:

2 ¼ cups all-purpose flour

¾ cup sugar

1 ¼ cups butter or margarine

¾ cup sour cream

2 eggs, beaten

½ teaspoon baking powder

½ teaspoon baking soda

¼ teaspoon salt

1 teaspoon almond extract

Filling:

1 package (8 ounces) cream
    cheese, softened

¼ cup sugar

1 egg, beaten

½ cup raspberry preserves*

½ cup sliced almonds

RASPBERRY-CHEESE COFFEE CAKE

Preheat oven to 350° F. Grease and flour bottom and sides of Springform Pan; set aside.

Prepare crust: Combine flour and 3/4 cup sugar in Batter Bowl. With Pastry Blender, cut in butter until mixture resembles coarse crumbs. Set aside 1 cup crumb mixture. To remaining crumb mixture, add sour cream, two eggs, baking powder, baking soda, salt and almond extract. Stir until smooth, then spread evenly over bottom and up 1 inch of sides in prepared pan.

Prepare filling: Mix cream cheese until smooth with 1/4 cup sugar and the remaining egg in Batter Bowl; pour into crust. Spoon preserves evenly over cream cheese mixture. Stir almonds into reserved crumb mixture and sprinkle over preserves. Bake 55 to 65 minutes, or until cream cheese filling is set and crust is golden brown. Cool to room temperature in Springform Pan, then release collar and remove. Serve warm, cut into wedges. Or refrigerate, covered in plastic wrap.

Yield: 16 servings

* Or substitute your favorite flavor preserves for raspberry.

Superbowl Party

If there's ever a time for hearty food, it's at a Superbowl Party. Yet it can't be too complicated, because the cook should be able to enjoy the game, too. These delicious, make-ahead recipes score on both accounts. Pull together the crunchy Party Mix and the Tamale Pie on Saturday night, and bake and frost the Football Cake on Sunday morning — a perfect buffet centerpiece. Use kids' helmets lined with heavy napkins to serve the snack mix. With fare like this and friends to share it, the party's sure to be a winner — no matter how the game turns out.

SUPERBOWL PARTY MIX

▪

TAMALE PIE

▪

SALAD OF ROMAINE WITH
ITALIAN DRESSING AND
CROUTONS

▪

FOOTBALL CAKE

10 cups unsalted popped
    popcorn*

2 cups unsalted pretzels

1 package (6 ounces) goldfish-
    shaped Cheddar cheese
    crackers

½ cup butter or margarine

⅔ cup grated Parmesan cheese

1 package (0.4 ounce) buttermilk
    recipe ranch dressing mix

1 garlic clove, pressed

SUPERBOWL PARTY MIX

Preheat oven to 350° F. In Baking Bowl, combine popcorn, pret-
zels and crackers; stir gently with Spoonula. In Microwave
Saucepan, melt butter (do not boil). To melted butter, add
Parmesan cheese, dressing mix and garlic; stir well with 10-inch
Whisk. Slowly pour butter mixture over popcorn mixture, stirring
constantly until popcorn mixture is evenly coated. Bake 15 minutes.

Yield: Approximately 14 cups

Variation: For Taco Party Mix, substitute 1 envelope (1¼ ounces)
taco spice and seasoning mix for ranch dressing mix and omit garlic.

* You may pop 1/2 cup popcorn kernels in 1/4 cup vegetable oil in covered Stir-Fry Skillet.
Or use 10 cups packaged popped popcorn, salted or unsalted.

---

1 pound lean ground beef

⅓ cup chopped green pepper

⅓ cup chopped onion

1 garlic clove, pressed

1 cup thick and chunky salsa, or
    1 can (8 ounces) tomato sauce

1 cup corn, fresh or frozen and
    thawed

1 envelope (1 ¼ ounces) taco
    spice and seasoning mix

1 package (8 ½ ounces) corn-
    bread mix

Milk (see label of corn-bread
    mix for amount)

Egg (see label of corn-bread
    mix for amount)

½ cup shredded Cheddar cheese

TAMALE PIE

Preheat oven to 375° F. In 10-inch Generation II Frying Pan, cook
ground beef, green pepper, onion and garlic, stirring often, until
beef is browned and crumbly. Drain off excess fat. Stir in salsa,
corn and taco seasoning. Spoon beef mixture into 8-inch Mini
Baker.

In Batter Bowl, stir corn-bread mix with milk and egg, according
to package directions, then spoon over beef mixture. Bake 35 to
40 minutes or until Cake Tester inserted in corn bread comes out
clean. Sprinkle corn-bread crust with cheese and bake another
minute or two, or until cheese is melted.

Yield: 4 servings

1 box (18 to 19 ounces) cake
   mix, any flavor

2 cups (8 ounces) shredded
   coconut

8 drops green food coloring

2 cups chocolate icing

½ cup vanilla icing

SUPER BATTER BOWL FOOTBALL CAKE

Preheat oven to 350º F. Grease and flour Batter Bowl, or spray with non-stick vegetable spray.

Prepare cake mix according to package directions, pour batter into prepared Batter Bowl, and bake 50 to 60 minutes, or until Cake Tester inserted in center of cake comes out clean. Cool cake in bowl on Non-Stick Cooling Rack 15 minutes, then invert bowl on rack and leave in place 3 to 4 hours for cake to release from bowl. Cool thoroughly before decorating.

To assemble: In clean Batter Bowl, toss coconut with food coloring until coconut is evenly tinted. Spread coconut evenly over oval serving platter. With Serrated Bread Knife, trim wide end of cake to make a flat surface for cake to rest on. Turn cake over to rest on flat bottom and slice in half vertically from narrow end at top to wide end at bottom. Arrange the halves on coconut with the two bottom surfaces pressed together; the two narrow ends will form the tips of the football. Spread with chocolate icing. Fill Decorating Set with vanilla icing and pipe "lacing" up center of football.

Yield: 12 to 15 servings

Winter Picnic

When the forecast says snow, plan a ... picnic! A winter picnic, that is, complete with cold-weather versions of all the foods you love to eat all summer long. The kids won't know what's going on, as they watch you spread a plaid blanket in the family room and pass out colorful paper plates and napkins. Chances are they'll soon get into the spirit, though, when they see what's for supper: Oven-Barbecued Ribs, baked beans, corn bread and adorable Ice Cream Cone Cupcakes. In fact, the only thing missing from this picnic is the ants!

OVEN-BARBECUED RIBS

■

BAKED BEANS

■

CORN BREAD

■

ICE CREAM CONE
CUPCAKES

■

APPLE JUICE

OVEN-BARBECUED RIBS

4 pounds pork spareribs

1 cup (8 ounces) bottled barbecue sauce

Preheat oven to 450° F. Cut spareribs into pieces of 3 or 4 ribs each and arrange in Deep Dish Baker. Cover with inverted Baking Bowl to create a covered baker. Bake 1 hour 30 minutes. Remove ribs to a platter, pour off and discard grease in baker. With Pastry Brush, brush ribs on all sides with sauce and arrange in baker. Reduce temperature to 250° F and bake, covered, 45 minutes longer.

Yield: 4 servings

ICE CREAM CONE CUPCAKES

1 box (18 to 19 ounces) cake mix, any flavor

24 to 30 flat-bottom cake-style ice cream cones

2 cups icing, any flavor

Toppings:

Chopped peanuts

Sprinkles

Mini chocolate chips

Preheat oven to 350° F. Prepare cake mix according to directions. Stand ice cream cones upright in Mini-Muffin Pans, and fill to within 1 inch of tops with cake batter. Bake 25 to 30 minutes, or until Cake Tester inserted in center comes out clean. Cool 15 minutes, then frost each cupcake with Icing Spreader and decorate with desired toppings.

Yield: 24 to 30 cone cupcakes.

Making the Cupcakes

1. Set flat-bottomed cake cones upright in Mini-Muffin Pan. Fill with cake batter to within 1 inch of tops.

2. Use Icing Spreader to spread icing over cooled cupcakes. Decorate as desired with candies and nuts.

Valentine's Sweets

Just when you need it most, Valentine's Day pops up to brighten that gray stretch of winter that seems to go on and on. Why not mark the occasion this year by giving homemade cookies to your favorite sweethearts? Thanks to packaged cookie dough, the Cookie Kisses and Giant Heart-Shaped Cookie couldn't be easier to make. The Cordial Cups are a little more involved, but well worth the effort. Tie bows of decorative red ribbon around cookie-filled cellophane bags for Valentine's gifts that are truly from the heart.

GIANT HEART-
SHAPED COOKIES

∎

COOKIE KISSES

∎

DOUBLE CHOCOLATE
CORDIAL CUPS

25

GIANT HEART-SHAPED COOKIES

1 package (20 ounces) refrigerated cookie dough, any flavor

Vanilla frosting, tinted pink

Pink or red decorator's sugar

Preheat oven to 350° F. Spray Heart-Shaped Insert of the Springform Pan set with non-stick vegetable spray; place Heart Insert on 15-inch Round Baking Stone and set aside. Divide dough into thirds and with lightly floured fingers, press 1/3 of dough evenly inside Heart-Shaped Insert. Bake 15 minutes or until cookie is crisp and golden. Cool 15 minutes on Baking Stone, then remove Insert from cookie; lift cookie onto Non-Stick Cooling Rack to finish cooling. Repeat to make two more cookies, or wrap and refrigerate dough for later use.

When cookies are thoroughly cool, decorate as desired using Decorating Set, pink icing and colored sugar.

COOKIE KISSES

1 package (20 ounces) refrigerated chocolate chip cookie dough

36 chocolate kisses, unwrapped

All-purpose flour

Preheat oven to 350° F. Lightly spray 3 Mini-Muffin Pans with non-stick vegetable spray and set aside. Cut dough into 9 thick slices, then cut each slice into 4 pieces, to make a total of 36 pieces. Place a piece of dough in each greased cup of Mini-Muffin Pans. Dip Mini-Tart Shaper in flour and press into dough to form cups. Reflour the Mini-Tart Shaper before forming each new cup. In each dough cup, place a chocolate kiss. Bake 10 to 12 minutes. Cool cookies in the pan 15 minutes, then remove to Non-Stick Cooling Rack to finish cooling.

Yield: 36 cookies

Crust:

1 package (8 ounces) cream cheese, softened

½ cup butter or margarine, softened

⅓ cup sugar

¾ cup all-purpose flour

¼ cup unsweetened cocoa powder

Filling:

¼ cup butter or margarine

6 tablespoons unsweetened cocoa powder

½ cup sugar

1 egg, beaten

1 teaspoon vanilla extract

1 tablespoon Grand Marnier liqueur

Double Chocolate Cordial Cups

Prepare crust: In Batter Bowl, combine cream cheese, butter and sugar; beat until fluffy. Sift together flour and cocoa; blend into cream cheese mixture until smooth. Divide and shape into 24 balls, then with Mini-Tart Shaper, press a ball into each cup of 2 ungreased Mini-Muffin Pans.

Prepare filling: Preheat oven to 325° F. Melt butter or margarine over low heat in 1½-quart Generation II Saucepan. Remove from heat. Stir in cocoa, then sugar, egg, vanilla and liqueur with Nylon Whisk. Spoon chocolate filling into crust-lined muffin cups, dividing evenly. Bake 25 to 30 minutes or until filling is set. Cool slightly in pan, then carefully remove with tip of paring knife. If desired, place in brightly colored paper liners to serve.

Yield: 24 cups

ardi Gras

At Mardi Gras time, the whole world is envious of the folks in New Orleans, for they seem to have more fun at their annual pre-Lenten celebration than the rest of us do all year long. But you don't have to go to Bourbon Street to join the party; you can throw a midweek festival in your own home by preparing this authentic Creole meal on Shrove Tuesday, the day before Lent begins. Feast on Crab Cakes, Jambalaya, a salad tossed with your favorite vinaigrette dressing, and a heady Pecan-Bourbon Bread Pudding. Add some peppy jazz or Cajun music, and you'll be dancing around the living room before you know it!

CRAB CAKES

▪

JAMBALAYA

▪

TOSSED GREEN SALAD

▪

PECAN-BOURBON
BREAD PUDDING

▪

COFFEE

2 cans (6 ounces each) crab
meat

2 eggs, lightly beaten

2 tablespoons bread crumbs

1 tablespoon milk

5 to 6 dashes hot red-pepper
sauce

1 lemon

2 teaspoons vegetable oil

½ cup cocktail sauce

New Orleans Crab Cakes

In Batter Bowl, combine crab meat, eggs, bread crumbs, milk and
red-pepper sauce. With Lemon Aid, squeeze 1/4 teaspoon lemon
juice into crab mixture, then toss lightly to mix.

Heat 1 teaspoon oil on 11-inch Square Griddle over medium-high
heat. Shape crab mixture into four patties and arrange on hot griddle. Cook 3 minutes, or until browned on bottom. Turn patties
and cook until browned on other side. Add remaining oil to griddle as necessary to prevent sticking. Serve crab cakes topped with
cocktail sauce.

Yield: 4 servings

1 cup chopped onion

1 cup chopped celery

1 tablespoon olive oil

8 ounces kielbasa or Cajun
sausage, casings removed,
coarsely chopped

3 garlic cloves, pressed

2 cups uncooked rice (not instant)

2 cans (16 ounces each)
chicken broth

1 can (14 ounces) quartered
artichoke hearts, drained

1 can (8 ounces) tomato sauce

1 ½ teaspoons dried thyme

1 teaspoon dried marjoram

1 ½ teaspoons hot red-pepper
sauce sauce

8 ounces shrimp, peeled and
deveined

1 cup chopped cooked chicken

½ cup finely chopped fresh
parsley (optional)

Chicken, Shrimp & Sausage Jambalaya

Using Food Chopper, chop and measure onion and celery. Heat
oil in Stir-Fry Skillet over medium heat. Add onion, celery and
sausage, and cook until onion is lightly browned, about 5 minutes.
Add garlic to sausage mixture and cook 1 minute. Stir in rice, then
chicken broth, artichoke hearts, tomato sauce, thyme, marjoram
and red-pepper sauce. Bring to a simmer, then turn heat to low.
Cover and cook 17 minutes, stirring occasionally. Add shrimp,
chicken and parsley. Cover and cook, stirring occasionally, 3 to 5
minutes or until shrimp are opaque and curled.

Yield: 6 to 8 servings

Custard:

2 teaspoons orange zest

¼ cup sugar

1 ½ cups milk

3 eggs

1 teaspoon vanilla extract

2 cups French bread cut in cubes

2 tablespoons bourbon (optional)

Topping:

½ cup pecans, chopped

2 tablespoons water

1 tablespoon bourbon (or water)

*1 tablespoon butter or
margarine*

*3 tablespoons brown sugar,
packed*

1 teaspoon molasses

PECAN-BOURBON BREAD PUDDING

Preheat oven to 300° F. Prepare custard: Scrape Lemon Zester/ Scorer across orange to make 2 teaspoons zest. Add zest to Batter Bowl with sugar, milk, eggs and vanilla. With 10-inch Whisk, whisk until foamy throughout. Divide bread cubes among 4 custard cups (6 ounces each), filling slightly less than half full. Pour custard mixture over bread to within 1/2 inch of tops. Place cups in 10-inch Generation II Frying Pan; fill pan with 1 ½ inches of warm water. Bake 1 to 1 ¼ hours or until firm. With 3-Way Tongs, remove cups from water bath. With Pastry Brush, brush hot pudding with the 2 tablespoons bourbon. Cool.

Prepare topping: Chop pecans with Food Chopper and set aside. In 1½-quart Generation II Saucepan, combine water, bourbon, butter, brown sugar and molasses. Bring to a boil over medium heat, stirring constantly. Add pecans, return topping to a boil, then remove from heat and spoon over pudding. Cool to serve.

Yield: 4 servings

Pasta Party

When you're not sure just how many are coming for that committee-meeting dinner, put pasta on the menu and you'll be safe no matter what. Make the elegant but easy Tiramisu the night before, assemble the bruschetta and the sauces just before the others arrive, and put the water on to boil for a couple of pounds of pasta. Then you can join the rest, knowing the crowd-pleasing dinner will be ready by the time you all need a break.

TOMATO BRUSCHETTA

∙

PASTA

∙

THE PERFECT
TOMATO SAUCE

∙

ALFREDO SAUCE

∙

TOSSED SALAD

∙

TIRAMISU

3 ripe, medium tomatoes,
   peeled, seeded and chopped

1 small onion, chopped

2 tablespoons chopped fresh
   basil or 2 teaspoons dried

1 garlic clove, pressed

¼ teaspoon salt

¼ teaspoon ground black pepper

1 baked loaf Canapé Bread
   (recipe, page 88) or 3 French
   baguettes

2 tablespoons olive oil

TOMATO BRUSCHETTA

Peel tomatoes with 3-inch Self-Sharpening Paring Knife, cut in half and gently squeeze out seeds. Chop tomatoes and onion with Food Chopper; place in Batter Bowl. Add basil to tomato-onion mixture. Press garlic with Garlic Press. Add garlic, salt and pepper to tomato mixture and stir well.

Preheat oven to 400° F. Slice bread into pieces 1/4-inch thick and arrange in single layer on 13-inch Round Baking Stone. Lightly brush slices of bread with oil. Bake 10 minutes or until lightly browned. Remove from oven, scoop a little tomato mixture on each slice of toast and serve warm.

Yield: 24 slices

1 medium onion, chopped

2 garlic cloves, pressed

1 teaspoon olive oil

2 cans (28 ounces each) Italian
   plum tomatoes, drained, juice
   reserved, and chopped

1 can (6 ounces) tomato paste

1 teaspoon dried basil

1 teaspoon dried oregano

2 bay leaves

Salt and ground black pepper
   to taste

1 package (16 ounces) pasta,
   cooked according to package
   directions

THE PERFECT TOMATO SAUCE

Chop onion with Food Chopper. Press garlic with Garlic Press. Combine onion, garlic and oil in 2-quart Generation II Saucepan. Cook over low heat, stirring frequently, 6 to 8 minutes or until onions are translucent. Chop tomatoes with Food Chopper. Add tomatoes with juice, tomato paste, basil, oregano and bay leaves to onion mixture. Bring to a simmer over medium heat. Reduce heat to low and cook 45 minutes, stirring frequently. Season with salt and pepper. Serve hot with cooked pasta.

Yield: 4 cups

2 cups (8 ounces) grated Parmesan cheese

1 ½ cups milk

1 ½ cups heavy cream

3 tablespoons butter or margarine

3 tablespoons all-purpose flour

Salt and ground white pepper to taste

1 package (16 ounces) pasta, cooked according to package directions

ALFREDO SAUCE

Combine milk and cream in 1½-quart Generation II Saucepan and heat until warm, about 120° F; do not boil. In 2-quart Generation II Saucepan, melt butter. Whisk in flour with Nylon Whisk. Pour heated milk and cream all at once into butter-flour mixture, whisking constantly. Bring to a simmer and cook, whisking constantly, until sauce is slightly thickened. Remove from heat and whisk in Parmesan cheese, salt and pepper. Toss while hot with drained hot pasta and serve immediately.

Yield: About 4 cups sauce

1 package (3.4 ounces) instant vanilla pudding mix

2 cups milk (or amount specified on pudding package label)

¼ cup light rum or cognac

¾ cup mascarpone cheese

1 pint heavy cream, whipped

12 ounces sponge cake, torn in bite-size pieces

1 cup strong espresso

1 tablespoon unsweetened cocoa powder

TIRAMISU

In Batter Bowl, combine pudding, milk and rum; mix well with 10-inch Whisk. Lighten the mascarpone cheese by turning and folding it over several times with Super Scraper, then mix into vanilla pudding. Fold in whipped cream to make filling.

To assemble, divide sponge cake pieces into three portions. Layer one third on bottom of Springform Pan or glass bowl. With Pastry Brush, drizzle sponge cake with 1/3 cup espresso; spread with a third of filling. Repeat twice to make three layers, using all of sponge cake, espresso and filling. Smooth surface of top layer. With Flour/Sugar Shaker, sprinkle cocoa over top. Cover pan with plastic wrap and refrigerate one hour or longer. Cut into wedges to serve.

Yield: 12 to 16 servings

Variation: Substitute ladyfingers (3-ounce package, 24 count) for the sponge cake.

Spring Fling *When the first crocus pokes its head through the cold ground, you know it's time for a big "welcome spring" party. Draw your neighbors out of hibernation by unfurling your daffodil house-banner and dusting off the recipes for some all-time favorite finger food: crispy Italian Potato Fingers, tidy Spinach Tarts made with the Cut-N-Seal, and tiny Herb & Cheese-Filled Cherry Tomatoes (the Tomato Corer and Cake Decorator make them easy). Dress the table with vases full of tulips, and watch springtime bloom inside your house, as well.*

ITALIAN POTATO
FINGERS

■

EASY SPINACH TARTS

■

HERB & CHEESE-
FILLED CHERRY
TOMATOES

■

BROWNIE-
CHEESECAKE BARS

■

ASSORTED CHEESES
AND CRACKERS

ITALIAN POTATO FINGERS

2 large baking potatoes

¼ cup butter or margarine, melted

1 package (0.7 ounce) dry Italian salad dressing mix

1 cup grated Parmesan cheese

Preheat oven to 400° F. Wash potatoes, leaving skin on. Slice potatoes in half lengthwise, then into quarters. Continue to cut quarters into thinner wedges. Combine melted butter and dry salad dressing mix in Batter Bowl; add potato fingers and toss to coat. Arrange potato fingers in single layer on 12" x 15" Rectangle Baking Stone and sprinkle with cheese. Bake 35 to 40 minutes or until crisp and browned. Serve warm or hot.

Yield: 4 to 6 servings

EASY SPINACH TARTS

1 package (10 ounces) frozen creamed spinach, thawed

18 to 20 slices soft-textured white or whole-wheat bread

¼ cup butter or margarine, melted

Preheat oven to 375° F. Place a scant teaspoon of spinach in center of a slice of bread. Gently fold bread in half to cover spinach. With 3-inch Cut-N-Seal, cut and seal to make crescent shape; brush lightly on both sides with melted butter. Repeat for additional tarts. Arrange in single layer on 12" x 15" Rectangle Baking Stone and bake 10 to 12 minutes or until golden brown.

Yield: 18 to 20 tarts

HERB & CHEESE-FILLED CHERRY TOMATOES

15 to 16 cherry tomatoes

1 package (3 ounces) cream cheese, softened

2 teaspoons All-Purpose Dill Mix

1 teaspoon milk

Dill sprigs for garnish (optional)

With Tomato Corer, remove tops and seeds from cherry tomatoes; turn hollowed tomatoes upside down on paper towels to drain a few minutes. In Batter Bowl, blend cream cheese, Dill Mix and milk with 10-inch Whisk until well blended and smooth. Fit Decorating Set with star tip and fill with cream cheese mixture. Pipe mixture into tomatoes to fill. Chill or serve immediately, garnished with dill sprigs.

Yield: 15 to 16 filled tomatoes

Brownies:

1 cup all-purpose flour

1 teaspoon baking powder

½ teaspoon salt

1 cup butter or margarine, softened

1 ⅔ cups sugar

3 eggs

4 ounces semisweet chocolate, melted and cooled

4 ounces unsweetened chocolate, melted and cooled

1 teaspoon vanilla extract

Cream Cheese Layer:

1 package (8 ounces) cream cheese, softened

½ cup sugar

1 egg, beaten

¼ cup sour cream

½ teaspoon vanilla extract

½ cup sliced almonds

BROWNIE-CHEESECAKE BARS

Preheat oven to 350° F. Prepare brownies: Lightly spray 9" x 13" Baker with non-stick vegetable spray and set aside. Mix flour with baking powder and salt; set aside. In mixing bowl, beat butter and sugar until light and fluffy. Add eggs, one at a time, beating well after each addition. Add melted chocolate and vanilla and mix well. Stir in dry ingredients and mix until well blended. Spread batter in prepared baker. Bake 10 minutes.

Prepare cream cheese layer: Meanwhile, beat cream cheese and sugar together until light and fluffy. Beat in egg, sour cream and vanilla. Spoon cream cheese mixture evenly over partially baked brownies, then sprinkle with almonds. Continue to bake 35 to 40 minutes, or until cream cheese layer is set. Cool completely in baker, then cut into bars.

Yield: 18 bars

Housewarming

Your family and friends are dying to see your new place, and you're dying to show it off (even if there is still a lot to do). Invite them for a tour and some hors d'oeuvres—nothing fancy, just crackers and cheese, hot and cold dips, crusty bread, vegetables and Mini-Ham Puffs, which look a lot harder to make than they are. You'll no doubt get lots of decorating tips throughout the day — but actually, the happy din of conversation, laughter and love will have already turned your house into a home.

MINI-HAM PUFFS

∎

CLASSIC DILL DIP

∎

HOT PIZZA DIP

∎

BREAD STICKS

∎

CRUDITÉS

∎

ASSORTED CHEESES
CRACKERS

1 package (2 ½ ounces)
  processed sliced ham

1 small onion

½ cup shredded Swiss cheese

1 egg, lightly beaten

1 ½ teaspoons Dijon-style
  mustard

⅛ teaspoon ground black
  pepper

1 package (8 ounces) refrigerated crescent rolls

MINI-HAM PUFFS

Preheat oven to 350° F. With Food Chopper, finely chop ham and onion; place in Batter Bowl with cheese, egg, mustard and pepper. Stir to combine; set aside.

Spray 2 Mini-Muffin Pans with non-stick vegetable spray. Unroll crescent-roll dough and press into a large rectangle, pinching seams to seal. Cut rectangle into 24 equal pieces with Pizza Cutter. Place dough pieces in Mini-Muffin Pan cups and with lightly floured Mini-Tart Shaper, press each piece into a cup shape. Dip Mini-Tart Shaper in flour as necessary to prevent sticking. With small Stainless Steel Scoop, divide the ham-cheese mixture evenly into dough cups. Bake 15 minutes or until lightly browned.

Yield: 24 appetizers

Variation: To create Mini-Ham Squares, spread dough on a 13-inch Round Baking Stone, pinching seams to seal. Spread ham mixture evenly over crust and bake at 350° F for 30 minutes or until lightly browned. To serve, cut into small squares with Pizza Cutter.

1 cup mayonnaise

1 cup sour cream

3 tablespoons All-Purpose Dill
  Mix

CLASSIC DILL DIP

Whisk mayonnaise, sour cream and Dill Mix together to blend well. Cover and chill for at least 1 hour or overnight. Serve with assorted crudités: raw vegetables such as cherry tomatoes, carrot and celery sticks, broccoli florets, cucumber rounds and bell pepper strips. Use the V-Shaped Cutter to create a red-pepper "dish" for the dip and the Lemon Zester/Scorer to dress up the crudités (see box at right).

1 package (8 ounces) cream
   cheese, softened

1 teaspoon Italian seasoning

1 cup shredded mozzarella
   cheese

¾ cup shredded Parmesan
   cheese

1 can (8 ounces) pizza sauce

2 tablespoons chopped green
   pepper

2 tablespoons chopped scallions

Bread sticks

HOT PIZZA DIP

Preheat oven to 350° F. In Batter Bowl, combine cream cheese and Italian seasoning. Mix well and spread over bottom of 8-inch Mini-Baker. Lightly toss mozzarella and Parmesan cheeses to mix and sprinkle half of grated cheeses over cream cheese. With Skinny Scraper, spread pizza sauce over cheeses. Top with remaining grated cheeses, peppers and scallions. Bake 15 to 18 minutes or until cheeses are melted and Pizza Dip is bubbling around the edges.*

Serve hot, with bread sticks that have been baked on the Baking Stone.

Yield: 12 servings

* Pizza Dip may also be heated in the microwave oven. Microwave on 100 percent power (high) for 2 minutes. Rotate and microwave 2 to 3 minutes longer, or until mixture is bubbly around edges.

Using the V-Shaped Cutter

For crown or zig-zag effect, cut through food by inserting V-Shaped Cutter repeatedly around perimeter.

Using the Lemon Zester/Scorer

To create a notched or grooved effect, pull Lemon Zester/Scorer down or across the surface of the food.

Bridal Shower

Of all the prenuptial traditions, the bridal shower may be the most treasured: Amid the whirlwind of wedding plans, the bride-to-be can relax for a while with the women closest to her, reveling in their excitement and best wishes. This luncheon menu — warm Potato-Chicken Salad, paired with a spinach salad and a lovely Lemon-Lime Mousse — certainly rises to the occasion. And wait until the guest of honor sees the beautiful, edible "Chapel" centerpiece, made with the Gingerbread House Mold. She may sign you up to do the wedding cake!

FRENCH POTATO-
CHICKEN SALAD

∎

SPINACH SALAD

∎

SMALL ROLLS

∎

QUICK LEMON-LIME
MOUSSE

∎

GINGERBREAD CHAPEL

FRENCH POTATO-CHICKEN SALAD

2 pounds unpeeled red potatoes, cut in ½-inch chunks

1 pound fresh green beans or 2 packages (10 ounces each) frozen, thawed, cut into 2-inch pieces

4 skinless, boneless chicken breast halves

½ cup olive oil

¼ cup white wine vinegar

2 tablespoons Dijon mustard

1½ teaspoons Worcestershire sauce

1 tablespoon All-Purpose Dill Mix

½ teaspoon salt

Ground black pepper to taste

Place potatoes in Stainless Steel Steamer. Cover and steam over medium heat for 10 minutes. Add beans to steamer, cover and steam 5 to 8 minutes longer, or until potatoes are tender. Transfer potatoes and beans to Batter Bowl and set aside to cool slightly.

Cut chicken into 1-inch cubes with 5-inch Self-Sharpening Utility Knife. Arrange chicken cubes in steamer, cover and steam 8 to 10 minutes, or until no trace of pink remains in center of cubes. Add chicken to Batter Bowl with vegetables.

In separate bowl, using Mini-Whipper, whisk oil with vinegar, mustard, Worcestershire sauce, Dill Mix, salt and pepper. Pour over chicken and vegetables and toss. Serve warm.

Yield: 12 servings

QUICK LEMON-LIME MOUSSE

1 ½ teaspoons lemon zest

1 ½ teaspoons lime zest

¾ cup lemon juice

3 tablespoons lime juice

9 egg yolks

1 ½ cups sugar

⅓ cup cornstarch

⅛ teaspoon salt

2 cups milk

3 cups heavy cream

Chill a stainless steel mixing bowl in the freezer. With Lemon Zester/Scorer, zest lemon and lime into 1½-quart Generation II Saucepan. Add lemon and lime juices to saucepan, along with egg yolks, sugar, cornstarch and salt. Using Nylon Whisk, whisk in milk and cook over medium heat, stirring constantly, until custard comes to a boil and is thickened, about 5 minutes.

Immediately pour custard into chilled stainless steel bowl and place a sheet of plastic wrap directly on surface of custard to prevent skin from forming. Quick-chill in freezer compartment, stirring occasionally, until custard begins to mound on spoon, about 30 minutes. (It should remain soft.)

When custard has cooled, whip cream in large mixing bowl until stiff peaks form. Fold whipped cream into the chilled custard using the Super Scraper. Spoon mousse into stemmed glasses or individual dessert bowls. Set on a tray, cover loosely with plastic wrap and refrigerate several hours or overnight. Serve chilled.

Yield: 12 servings

Gingerbread Base:

3 cups all-purpose flour

1 ½ teaspoons ground cinnamon

1 teaspoon ground ginger

¼ teaspoon ground cloves

¼ teaspoon salt

½ cup butter, softened*

½ cup sugar

½ cup molasses

1 egg yolk

GINGERBREAD CHAPEL

(For correct number of pieces, bake two batches of each section of the Stoneware Gingerbread House Mold except chimney, which requires only one section. This recipe is sufficient for both batches.)

Preheat oven to 350° F. Prepare gingerbread base: Lightly spray Gingerbread Mold with non-stick vegetable spray; blot up excess oil with paper towel. Set aside.

Stir flour with cinnamon, ginger, cloves and salt; set aside. In a large mixing bowl, beat butter and sugar with an electric mixer at high speed until light and fluffy. Add molasses and egg yolk and beat until smooth. With mixer on low speed, gradually add flour mixture and beat until dough is well blended. (Dough will be stiff and slightly dry.)

Shape dough into a large ball, then divide in half. Wrap one half of dough in plastic wrap; set aside. Press remaining dough firmly into greased mold. Level and smooth the dough with Serrated Bread Knife. Bake 20 minutes or until lightly browned. Place Non-Stick Cooling Rack over mold, then invert mold and cooling rack together to unmold gingerbread pieces directly onto rack. Cool mold completely before baking remaining dough. Lightly spray mold again with non-stick vegetable spray before refilling.

* Do not substitute margarine for butter in this recipe.

Royal Icing:

(This sticky frosting acts as the "mortar" that holds the chapel together.)

1 ¼ cups confectioners' sugar

1 egg white

⅛ teaspoon cream of tartar

Prepare the Royal Icing: Place all ingredients in small, nonplastic mixing bowl. Beat first on low speed until sugar is incorporated, then beat on high speed until frosting is glossy and holds peaks, about 5 minutes. This frosting dries very quickly; cover with plastic wrap when not in use. If desired, tint frosting with food coloring before use.

Yield: approximately 1 cup

(If you are covering large areas of the chapel with frosting, you may need to make two batches.)

Assembling the Gingerbread Chapel

1. Pipe Royal Icing around sides of walls. Press walls together and let dry 5 to 10 minutes.

2. Pipe icing along tops of walls. Gently press roof pieces along frosted edges and let dry 5 to 10 minutes.

3. With 3-inch Self-Sharpening Paring Knife, cut chimney into steeple shape, about 2 inches tall.

4. Spread steeple with icing and affix to one end of chapel roof. Decorate chapel as desired with icing, mints, and other small candies.

Mother's Day Breakfast in Bed

You'll know something's up when you smell coffee brewing and bacon sizzling, but go along with it — and you'll be rewarded with a delicious meal and some very proud children (to say nothing of an extra few minutes' sleep). The Baked Apple French Toast is easy enough for the kids to do (with a little help from Dad) but a bit elegant, too; it's the perfect special recipe for the special woman in their lives. They will be bursting with excitement and pride when they see your eyes well up at this simple but touching display of their gratitude for all you do for them all year long.

BAKED APPLE
FRENCH TOAST

•

MAPLE SYRUP

•

FRESH STRAWBERRIES

•

CRISP BACON

1 large loaf or 2 small loaves
French bread

8 eggs

3 cups milk

¾ cup sugar

1 tablespoon vanilla extract

5 Granny Smith apples

2 teaspoons ground cinnamon

2 tablespoons butter or
margarine

BAKED APPLE FRENCH TOAST

Preheat oven to 400° F. Spray 9" x 13" Baker lightly with non-stick vegetable spray. Cut bread into 1 ½-inch slices with Serrated Bread Knife and arrange closely in a single layer in Baker. In Batter Bowl, beat eggs lightly. Beat in milk, 1/4 cup of the sugar, and vanilla using 10-inch Whisk. Pour half of egg-milk mixture over bread.

Peel, core and slice apples with Apple Peeler/Corer/Slicer. Arrange apple rings evenly over bread in Baker; pour remaining egg-milk mixture over apples. Mix remaining 1/2 cup of sugar with cinnamon in Flour/Sugar Shaker. Sprinkle evenly over apples, then dot with butter.* Bake 35 minutes. Cool 5 to 10 minutes, then cut into squares and serve with maple syrup.

Yield: 12 servings

(For 6 servings, divide recipe in half and bake in Deep Dish Baker about 20 minutes.)

*Baked Apple French Toast can be prepared ahead to this point, covered with plastic wrap, and refrigerated overnight, then baked for 50 minutes the next morning.

Last Day of School

Remember the electricity in the air on the last day of school? Recreate that exhilaration, that sense of accomplishment, that excitement about the long, lazy days that lie ahead with a menu that offers the warm-weather eating you love. Even if you don't have kids or haven't been in class yourself in years, you're sure to enjoy celebrating the beginning of summer with spicy El Paso Burgers, jazzed up for the grill with taco seasoning, onions and peppers, and topped with cheese and a dollop of sour cream. Finish off with the cool, colorful Watermelon Bombe, made with three different sherbets and studded with clever chocolate chip "seeds."

EL PASO BURGERS

▪

COLESLAW

▪

CHIPS

▪

WATERMELON BOMBE

1 medium onion, chopped

1 small green pepper, chopped

2 pounds lean ground beef

1 package (1 ¼ ounces) taco seasoning mix

8 ounces Monterey Jack cheese with hot peppers, sliced

½ cup sour cream

½ cup chunky salsa

8 hamburger buns

EL PASO BURGERS

Chop onion and green pepper finely with Food Chopper. Add to ground beef along with taco seasoning mix and mix well with Bamboo Spoon. Shape beef mixture into eight patties. Grill or fry to desired doneness; use Bar-B-Boss to turn patties once during cooking. When patties are cooked, top each with a slice of hot pepper cheese and about 1 tablespoon each of sour cream and salsa. Arrange on hamburger buns and serve immediately.

Yield: 8 burgers

(Patties may be formed and frozen for later use, separated by squares of Kitchen Parchment Paper.)

1 ½ pints lime sherbet

1 pint lemon or pineapple sherbet

1 ½ quarts raspberry sherbet, softened

¼ cup chocolate chips

WATERMELON BOMBE

Chill Batter Bowl in freezer for 30 minutes. Press lime sherbet over bottom and sides of chilled Batter Bowl; return to freezer until sherbet is very firm, about 45 minutes. Press lemon or pineapple sherbet over lime sherbet and freeze until very firm. In a separate bowl, blend softened raspberry sherbet with chocolate chips. Spoon into sherbet-lined Batter Bowl to form center of "watermelon" and freeze until very firm, at least 2 hours.

To serve: Invert Batter Bowl on chilled serving plate and wrap a warm, wet towel around bowl to loosen and release the sherbet. Remove Batter Bowl. Slice Watermelon Bombe into wedges and serve immediately.

Variation: Substitute vanilla ice cream, tinted the appropriate color, for one of the sherbets.

Yield: 14 to 16 wedges

Birthday Cake Surprises

For the next birthday in your house, don't just bake a cake...bake a baseball cap, trimmed in your child's school colors or those of your child's favorite pro team. Or choose a clown, a happy, colorful guy with candy for his features and the same party hat the kids have on. You can even bake a fashion doll cake — only you will know how you were able to make her lavish pink ball gown without getting frosting on her legs. With the multipurpose Batter Bowl, these creations are "a piece of cake."

1 box (18 to 19 ounces) cake
  mix, any flavor

3 ½ cups vanilla icing

Food coloring

Gum drop

BASEBALL CAP CAKE

Preheat oven to 350° F. Grease and flour Batter Bowl or lightly spray with non-stick vegetable spray. Prepare cake batter according to package directions and pour into prepared Batter Bowl. Bake 55 to 65 minutes, or until Cake Tester inserted in center of cake comes out clean. Cool cake in bowl 15 minutes on Non-Stick Cooling Rack, then invert bowl on rack and leave in place 3 to 4 hours for cake to release from bowl. Cool thoroughly before decorating.

To assemble: Trim off rounded bottom of cake with Serrated Bread Knife to level. Slice a 1-inch base from widest part of cake and using Batter Bowl as guide, cut out a crescent shape to form bill of cap (about half of the cake slice). Discard remaining portion of slice. Arrange dome-shaped part of cake on serving tray, cut side down, and push crescent-shaped piece against rounded side of cake to form bill of cap. Tint 2 cups icing desired color and spread over top of cap. Tint 1 cup of remaining icing in a contrasting color and spread over bill of cap. Tint remaining 1/2 cup icing in a third color, and using Decorating Set, decorate cake. Place gum drop on top of cap for button.

Yield: 12 to 15 servings

1 box (18 to 19 ounces) cake
  mix, any flavor

4 cups vanilla icing

5 2½-inch cookies, cut in half

Gum ball and gum drops

Food coloring

1 paper party hat

CLOWN CAKE

Preheat oven to 350° F. Grease and flour Batter Bowl or lightly spray with non-stick vegetable spray. Prepare cake batter according to package directions and pour into prepared Batter Bowl. Bake 55 to 65 minutes, or until cake tester inserted in center of cake comes out clean. Cool cake in bowl 15 minutes on Non-Stick Cooling Rack, then invert bowl on rack and leave in place 3 to 4 hours for cake to release from bowl. Cool thoroughly before decorating.

To assemble: Trim off rounded bottom of cake with Serrated Bread Knife to level. Set cake on serving tray, cut side down, and spread with 2 cups of the vanilla icing. Arrange cookies around bottom of cake for ruffled collar. Tint 1 cup of icing orange, 1/2 cup red, and 1/2 cup green. With Decorating Set, pipe orange icing for hair and pipe red and green icing to complete clown face as shown. Use gum drops and gum ball for eyes and nose. Top with party hat.

Yield: 12 to 15 servings

2 boxes (18 to 19 ounces each)
  cake mix, any flavor

4 cups vanilla icing

Food coloring

DOLL CAKE

Preheat oven to 350° F. Grease and flour 2 Batter Bowls or lightly spray with non-stick vegetable spray. Prepare 2 batches of cake batter according to package directions and pour into prepared Batter Bowls. Bake 55 to 65 minutes, or until Cake Tester inserted in center of cake comes out clean. Cool cakes in bowls 15 minutes on Non-Stick Cooling Rack, then invert bowls. Cool 3 to 4 hours before decorating.

Assembling the Doll Cake

1. Test for doneness by inserting Cake Tester into center of cake. Cool cakes in Batter Bowls 15 minutes on Cooling Rack, then invert. Cool 3 to 4 hours before decorating.

2. With Serrated Bread Knife, slice off 2 inches from bottom of one cake to lengthen doll's skirt; arrange on cake plate. Set second cake on 2-inch base.

3. With Apple Corer, scoop out center of cake and insert doll, wrapped in plastic wrap from waist down.

4. Decorate with tinted icing, using the Decorating Set.

To assemble: With Serrated Bread Knife, trim off rounded bottoms of cakes to level. Slice off 2 inches from bottom of one cake and arrange on serving tray or platter to serve as bottom of doll's skirt. (Wrap and freeze unused top portion of first cake for later use, or frost and serve with Doll Cake, if more servings are needed.)

Position second cake on top of 2-inch cake base. "Core" through center of cake with Apple Corer to make a well large enough for doll. Wrap undressed doll from waist down in plastic wrap and insert into well.

Tint 3 cups of icing pink and spread over cake and bodice area of doll. Tint remaining icing violet or another contrasting color. Using Decorating Set, decorate doll's "dress." To serve, remove doll and cut cake into slices.

Yield: 12 to 15 servings

make Your Own Pizza

If your house is charged with lots of pent-up energy, try putting the kids to work as pizza chefs. They'll love all the mixing and measuring, kneading and punching...and they'll be amazed when the dough doubles in just an hour! In the meantime, throw together a big batch of sauce, cut up some toppings (everyone gets to pick their own), and let the kids spread it all over the fresh crust. Your chefs will be thrilled with their creations — and should have just enough energy left to eat!

HOMEMADE PIZZA
CRUST
HOMEMADE PIZZA
SAUCE

■

ASSORTED TOPPINGS
INCLUDING:
MOZZARELLA CHEESE,
PARMESAN CHEESE, PEP-
PERONI, GREEN PEPPER,
MUSHROOMS, HAM,
PINEAPPLE, ONION AND
COOKED SAUSAGE

⅔ cup lukewarm water
(105°-115° F)

1 ½ teaspoons active dry yeast
(½ package)

2 ¼ cups plus 2 tablespoons
all-purpose flour

¾ teaspoon salt

2 tablespoons olive oil

Additional oil

PIZZA CRUST (FOR 1 PIZZA)

Stir water and yeast in small bowl, then set aside until yeast is dissolved, about 5 minutes. Meanwhile, combine 2 ¼ cups flour and salt in Batter Bowl. Make a well in center and pour in yeast mixture and oil. Stir with Bamboo Spoon until dough forms a ball. Turn onto floured work surface. If dough is too sticky to handle, sprinkle with remaining 2 tablespoons flour. Knead dough until smooth and elastic, about 5 minutes. Turn into clean Batter Bowl brushed with additional oil, turning to oil dough on all sides. Cover with damp towel and set in warm place until about double in size, about 1 hour.

When dough has doubled, preheat oven to 475° F. Punch dough down, place on 13-inch Round Baking Stone and roll into a 12-inch circle. Spread each pizza with about 1 cup Pizza Sauce and top with your favorite pizza toppings. Bake 17 to 20 minutes, or until crust is golden brown. Cut into wedges with the Pizza Cutter and serve.

Yield: 6 servings

2 pounds fresh tomatoes, peeled
and chopped, juices reserved,
or 1 can (28 ounces) Italian
plum tomatoes and their juice

4 garlic cloves, pressed

2 tablespoons olive oil

½ teaspoon red pepper flakes
(optional)

¼ teaspoon dried basil

¼ teaspoon dried oregano

Salt and ground black pepper
to taste

PIZZA SAUCE

With Food Chopper, coarsely chop fresh tomatoes, if using, and set aside. Press garlic with Garlic Press into 2-quart Generation II Saucepan. Stir in olive oil, red pepper flakes, basil and oregano, and cook over medium heat 1 to 2 minutes. Add tomatoes and their juice, bring to a simmer and cook uncovered, stirring occasionally, 25 to 35 minutes or until sauce is thickened. Season with salt and pepper. The sauce can be used immediately or stored in an air-tight container in the refrigerator for up to 1 week.

Yield: 2 cups (enough for 2 pizzas)

Late-Night Dinner for Two

When the children are small it can be tough to squeeze in a spontaneous evening out to celebrate a promotion or other unexpected good luck. But don't let the important times pass by unnoticed; plan an intimate, late-night dinner for two...in your own home. One of you can bathe the kids while the other gets the rice going and pulls together the Pork and Spinach Salad. After you've tucked in the little ones, you can settle down to savor some sophisticated food at a leisurely pace — and toast your happiness together.

PORK AND SPINACH
STIR-FRY SALAD

■

PECAN RICE

■

BREAD

■

LEMON SUGAR
COOKIES WITH
SORBET

53

½ package (5 ounces) fresh
spinach leaves, stemmed,
washed and drained

1 can (11 ounces) mandarin
oranges, drained

2 tablespoons white wine vinegar

2 teaspoons fresh lemon juice

1 tablespoon sugar

¼ teaspoon dry mustard

¼ teaspoon salt

White pepper to taste

¼ cup vegetable oil

½ pound boneless pork loin, cut
in thin strips (⅜-inch wide)

¼ cup thinly sliced scallions

¼ cup slivered almonds, toasted
lightly

PORK AND SPINACH STIR-FRY SALAD

Tear spinach in bite-size pieces and arrange on serving platter or
in large shallow salad bowl. Top with mandarin orange sections;
set aside. In small bowl, whisk together vinegar, lemon juice,
sugar, dry mustard, salt and white pepper; whisk oil slowly into
mixture and set aside.

Spray Stir-Fry Skillet with non-stick vegetable spray and place
over high heat 1 to 2 minutes to preheat. Add pork and scallions
and stir-fry until no trace of pink remains in meat, 4 to 5 minutes.
Add oil-vinegar mixture to pork and green scallions and cook
another minute, or until heated through.

Spoon pork and dressing over spinach and mandarin orange
sections, toss gently, sprinkle with slivered almonds and serve.

Yield: 2 servings

---

1 cup condensed chicken broth

½ cup uncooked rice (not
instant)

1 tablespoon vegetable oil

¼ cup pecans, chopped

2 thinly sliced scallions

1 small garlic clove, pressed

½ teaspoon grated fresh ginger

½ cup fresh mushrooms, sliced

½ medium red pepper, thinly
sliced

½ cup frozen green peas, thawed

½ teaspoon orange zest

1 egg, beaten

PECAN RICE

In 2-quart Generation II Saucepan, bring chicken broth to a boil.
Stir in rice and reduce heat to simmer. Cover and cook 20 minutes.

Meanwhile, heat oil in Stir-Fry Skillet. Add pecans, scallions, garlic
and ginger; stir-fry on medium high 2 minutes. Add mushrooms
and red pepper; stir-fry 3 minutes. Stir in cooked rice, peas and
orange zest. Push rice mixture to sides of skillet to expose the
center of skillet. Pour beaten egg into center of skillet, cook until
egg is set, then rapidly stir into rice mixture. Serve hot.

Yield: 2 servings

2 cups all-purpose flour

½ teaspoon baking soda

½ teaspoon cream of tartar

¼ teaspoon salt

½ cup butter or margarine,
  softened

1 teaspoon grated lemon zest

½ teaspoon vanilla extract

1 cup plus 2 tablespoons sugar

1 egg

2 tablespoons milk

LEMON SUGAR COOKIES

In a small bowl, stir flour with baking soda, cream of tartar and salt. In Batter Bowl, cream butter with Bamboo Spoon. Add lemon zest, vanilla and 1 cup sugar, and mix well. Stir in egg and milk. Gradually add dry ingredients, blending after each addition until dough is smooth. Turn dough out onto plastic wrap and shape into a log. Refrigerate dough, wrapped in plastic wrap, at least 2 hours or overnight.

Preheat oven to 375° F. Cut chilled dough log into thirds; return two portions, wrapped in plastic wrap, to refrigerator. On lightly floured surface, roll one portion of dough to 1/8-inch thickness, using Dough and Pizza Roller. With Star-Shaped Valtrompia Bread Tube, cut cookies into star shapes and arrange on 15-inch Round Baking Stone. Gather, roll and cut any dough scraps into cookies. Bake 10 to 12 minutes, or until edges begin to brown. Transfer cookies to Non-Stick Cooling Rack and sprinkle while warm with some of the remaining 2 tablespoons sugar.

Repeat rolling and baking with remaining two portions of dough. Cool cookies completely, then store in airtight container.

Yield: about 3 dozen cookies

Fourth of July Cookout

Trying to jazz up that reliable old Independence Day tradition, the backyard barbecue? Start with the always-popular deviled eggs, dressed up with tiny shrimp and chives. Then, for a change from burgers and dogs, grill tasty chicken and vegetable kebabs. Later, as the fireworks are exploding, light some sparklers on your dazzling dessert — a pizza topped with blueberry "stars" and strawberry and banana "stripes" — and watch them burn brightly as you all celebrate America's birthday.

GRILLED CHICKEN &
VEGETABLE KEBABS

SHRIMP DEVILED EGGS

CORN ON THE COB

STARS AND STRIPES
DESSERT PIZZA

2 garlic cloves, pressed

½ cup olive oil

1 tablespoon chopped fresh
oregano or ½ teaspoon dried

2 teaspoons chopped fresh basil
or 1 teaspoon dried

1 teaspoon salt

½ teaspoon ground black pepper

1 ½ pounds skinless, boneless
chicken breasts, cut in 1-inch
pieces

2 medium zucchini, cut in 1-inch
pieces

1 medium green pepper, cut in
1-inch squares

16 cherry tomatoes

16 medium mushroom caps

GRILLED CHICKEN & VEGETABLE KEBABS

Prepare coals for barbecue. Press garlic into Batter Bowl using Garlic Press. Whisk in oil, oregano, basil, salt and pepper. Divide chicken, zucchini and green pepper pieces into 8 equal portions and thread alternately onto eight 10-inch metal skewers. Allot 2 cherry tomatoes and 2 mushrooms for each skewer, beginning and ending with a mushroom. With Pastry Brush, brush chicken and vegetables liberally with the oil-herb mixture.

Grill kebabs 4 inches from heat source, turning frequently, until chicken is firm and vegetables are tender, about 10 minutes. During grilling, brush kebabs occasionally with oil-herb mixture. Serve hot.

Yield: 8 servings

12 large eggs, hard cooked and
shelled

¾ cup mayonnaise

½ teaspoon dry mustard

¼ teaspoon salt

1 can (4 ¼ ounces) or 1 bag
(5 ounces) frozen cooked baby
shrimp

1 tablespoon chopped fresh chives

SHRIMP DEVILED EGGS

With Garnisher, cut eggs in half lengthwise, using a circular motion to create a swirl pattern on surface of eggs. Remove yolks to small mixing bowl and crumble with fork. Add mayonnaise, dry mustard and salt, and mix until smooth.

Set aside 24 whole shrimp. With Pastry Blender, flake remaining shrimp in small bowl, then stir into yolk mixture. Fill egg white halves with shrimp-yolk mixture, dividing evenly among the 24 whites. Top each deviled egg with a whole shrimp and sprinkle with chives. Arrange on serving platter, cover with plastic wrap and refrigerate until ready to serve.

Yield: 24 deviled egg halves

1 ½ (8 ounces each)
  packages refrigerated
  crescent rolls

1 package (8 ounces)
  cream cheese, softened

1 cup confectioners' sugar

1 teaspoon lemon zest

1 teaspoon lemon juice

1 to 2 pints strawberries,
  hulled, washed and
  drained

1 cup blueberries, washed
  and drained

2 medium bananas*

Lemon-lime soda or addi-
  tional lemon juice

STARS AND STRIPES DESSERT PIZZA

Preheat oven to 350° F. Unroll refrigerated crescent-roll dough into 3 long strips. Arrange dough over 12" x 15" Rectangle Baking Stone to cover, pinching seams together to seal. Bake 15 minutes or until golden brown. Remove from oven and cool to room temperature.

In mixer bowl, beat cream cheese until fluffy. Add confectioners' sugar, lemon zest and lemon juice; beat on low speed until smooth. Spread evenly over cooled crust. Spread strawberries and blueberries on paper towels to blot water. With Egg Slicer, slice strawberries and bananas. Immediately dip banana slices in lemon-lime soda to prevent browning.

To assemble: Arrange blueberries over upper left-hand corner of crust to represent stars. Make alternating rows of strawberries and bananas to represent stripes. Cover with plastic wrap and chill up to 6 hours.

When ready to serve, make 3 cuts down and 3 cuts across with Pizza Cutter to form 16 rectangles.

Yield: 16 servings

* If desired, omit bananas, leaving open rows between strawberries to represent white stripes.

58

It's Too Hot to Cook

No one wants to eat a hot, heavy meal when the mercury and humidity are sky-high. And you sure don't want to cook one. Instead, chop up some celery and turkey from the deli, open some cans of corn and beans, and toss it all together with a spicy Southwestern dressing for a light but satisfying salad. For a cool ending, dip into homemade Creamy Orange Ice, a happy throwback to the confection we all loved as kids. It's a breeze to create with the Ice Shaver.

SOUTHWEST TURKEY
SALAD

∙

TORTILLA CHIPS

∙

CARROT STICKS

∙

CREAMY ORANGE ICE

∙

LEMONADE

Dressing:

⅔ cup mild salsa

½ cup sour cream

1 tablespoon ground cumin

¾ teaspoon salt

½ teaspoon ground black pepper

Salad:

1 can (15 ounces) kidney beans

1 can (17 ounces) corn kernels

2 cups (8 ounces) cooked turkey cut in ½-inch cubes

3 celery stalks, diced

8 lettuce leaves, shredded

2 cups tortilla chips

SOUTHWEST TURKEY SALAD

Prepare dressing: In small bowl whisk together salsa, sour cream, cumin, salt and pepper. Cover and refrigerate briefly while you make the salad.

Prepare salad: Place kidney beans in colander and rinse under cold running water. Add corn and drain well. With 5-inch Self-Sharpening Utility Knife, cut turkey into 1/2-inch cubes. Place beans and corn in Batter Bowl, add turkey and celery, and toss lightly to mix.

To serve: Arrange lettuce on 4 dinner plates. Spoon a quarter of the turkey salad over lettuce on each plate and garnish with tortilla chips. Serve dressing on the side.

Yield: 4 servings

1 can (6 ounces) frozen orange juice concentrate, thawed

2 cups half-and-half

½ cup water

⅓ cup sugar

1 tablespoon vanilla extract

CREAMY ORANGE ICE

Place juice concentrate, half-and-half, water, sugar and vanilla in Batter Bowl. Mix with 10-inch Whisk until sugar is dissolved. Divide evenly among 3 Ice Shaver Tubs and freeze until firm. Remove from tubs and shave in the Ice Shaver. Pile Creamy Orange Ice into stemmed glasses or dessert bowls. Garnish with candied orange slices, if desired, and serve with a spoon.

Yield: 6 servings

Variation: For a lighter version, substitute 2 cups evaporated skim milk for the half-and-half and prepare as directed.

Family Movie Night

Looking for an easy, inexpensive way for the whole family to have a night out at the movies? Try staying in! The seats are more comfortable, the beverages are free, and the chicken and vegetable stir-fry is better than any you'd get from the take-out place. So whip up a big bowl of popcorn for later, slip a comedy or classic into the VCR, and settle in on the couch. Family Night at the Movies may become your favorite Friday night tradition!

EGG ROLLS

■

SOUTHERN STIR-FRY

■

STEAMED RICE

■

FORTUNE COOKIES

■

POPCORN

■

ICED TEA

1 pound boneless, skinless
chicken breasts

¼ teaspoon ground ginger

⅛ teaspoon salt

⅛ teaspoon ground black pepper

⅔ cup condensed chicken broth

2 tablespoons cornstarch

2 tablespoons soy sauce

1 tablespoon water

½ teaspoon sugar

1 tablespoon vegetable oil

1 garlic clove, thinly sliced

1 medium onion, thinly sliced

2 medium carrots, peeled and
cut with Garnisher

1 can (15 ounces) baby corn-on-
the-cob, drained

1 cup (about 5 ounces) fresh
green beans, stemmed

1 medium red pepper, seeded,
thinly sliced

2 cups hot cooked rice

SOUTHERN STIR-FRY

Cut chicken breasts into strips about 2 inches long and 1/4-inch thick. In small bowl, mix together ginger, salt and pepper; sprinkle over chicken strips. In another bowl, combine chicken broth, cornstarch, soy sauce, water and sugar; set within easy reach of rangetop.

Heat oil in Stir-Fry Skillet over high heat. Add chicken strips and garlic; stir-fry 3 to 4 minutes. Add onion, carrots, corn, green beans and red pepper; stir-fry 4 to 5 minutes. Stir in broth-corn-starch mixture and cook, stirring, until thickened. Serve immediately over hot cooked rice.

Yield: 4 servings

Using the Garnisher

For decorative sticks or rounds, cut foods with rocking motion of Garnisher. Keep end closest to your body firmly anchored on cutting board.

Breakfast for Dinner

When you want a change of pace but don't have a particular reason to celebrate, turn dinnertime upside down and serve breakfast! Not just bowls of cold cereal, mind you. We're talking apple pancakes and country ham and bacon-egg tarts — the kind of hearty fare you rarely have time to enjoy on busy mornings. Let the kids sit in your chair, while you sit in theirs. They'll march off to bed with a bounce in their step, thanks to the fun-loving way you transformed a ho-hum weeknight into a memorable occasion.

MENU 1
CINNAMON APPLE
PANCAKES

■

COUNTRY HAM OR BACON

■

ORANGE JUICE

■

MENU 2
MELON SALAD WITH
ORANGE-LIME DRESSING

■

BREAKFAST TARTS

■

MILK

63

1 Granny Smith apple

1 cup pancake mix (any variety)

½ teaspoon ground cinnamon

1 cup milk

1 egg, lightly beaten

1 tablespoon plus 2 teaspoons vegetable oil

CINNAMON APPLE PANCAKES

Using the Apple Peeler/Corer/Slicer, peel, core and slice the apple into rings. In Batter Bowl, combine pancake mix and cinnamon. Add milk, egg and 1 tablespoon of oil; stir just to mix. Add a little more milk or water if necessary to make batter thin enough to pour easily.

Preheat 11-inch Square Griddle on medium-high heat until drop of water dances on surface; quickly rub 1/4 to 1/2 teaspoon oil onto griddle using a crumpled paper towel. Spray the inner rim of pancake molds with non-stick vegetable spray and set on griddle. Place an apple ring in the middle of each mold. Slowly pour about 1/4 cup batter over the apple ring, starting in the center. Use just enough batter to cover the apple ring and fill mold.

Cook until pancakes begin to look dry on top, then remove molds and turn pancakes with broad spatula. Continue to cook until lightly browned on other side. (If batter sticks to spatula, wipe clean with the oiled paper towel.) Repeat until all the batter has been cooked, greasing griddle as necessary with remaining oil. Serve hot, with butter and maple syrup.

Yield: 8 to 10 pancakes

1 lime

2 tablespoons frozen orange or
tangerine juice concentrate,
thawed

¼ teaspoon vanilla extract or
ground coriander

½ cantaloupe

½ honeydew melon

1 ½ cups seedless red grapes

MELON SALAD WITH ORANGE-LIME DRESSING

With Lemon Zester/Scorer, remove 1 teaspoon zest from lime and place in Batter Bowl. With Lemon Aid, squeeze 3 tablespoons lime juice into Batter Bowl with the zest. Stir in orange juice concentrate and vanilla or coriander.

With 5-inch Self-Sharpening Utility Knife, slice each melon half into wedges about 1 inch wide. Trim away rind and cut each wedge into 3/4-inch cubes. Add melon cubes and grapes to Batter Bowl with lime dressing and toss lightly to coat. Cover with Batter Bowl lid and chill at least 2 hours before serving.

Yield: 4 servings

2 large eggs, scrambled

¼ cup cooked Canadian bacon,
finely chopped

¼ cup shredded Cheddar cheese

32 slices soft-textured white or
whole-wheat bread

Melted butter or margarine

BREAKFAST TARTS

Preheat oven to 375° F. In Batter Bowl, mix scrambled eggs with Canadian bacon and cheese. To make Breakfast Tarts, place a scant tablespoon of egg-bacon mixture on center of a bread slice

and top with another slice of bread. Use the 3-inch Cut-N-Seal to cut and seal round Breakfast Tart. Lightly brush both sides with melted butter, then place on 15-inch Round Baking Stone. Repeat for additional Breakfast Tarts. Bake 10 to 12 minutes, or until lightly toasted.

Yield: 16 tarts

Back-to-School Lunches

A new school year, a new beginning — for the lunchbox, too! Try a few quick and healthy changes that will brighten everyone's noontime: For example, slip grated carrot into tuna salad or crunchy sunflower seeds into cream cheese. Choose breads made with whole-wheat flour instead of white. Make your kids smile by sealing their sandwiches in new shapes with the Cut-N-Seal. Tuck in a few carrot, celery or zucchini sticks cut with the Garnisher, and close with colorful Twixits clips, for school lunches your children wouldn't dream of trading.

TUNA-CARROT SALAD
PITA POCKETS
▪
TURKEY-APPLE SALAD
SANDWICHES
▪
PEANUT BUTTER OR
SOFTENED CREAM
CHEESE WITH:
CRUMBLED BACON,
GRATED CARROTS,
JAM OR JELLY,
SHREDDED COCONUT,
CHOPPED DRIED
APRICOTS, SHELLED
SUNFLOWER SEEDS

66

TUNA-CARROT SALAD PITA POCKETS

1 can (6 ½ ounces) water-packed white tuna, drained

1 medium carrot, coarsely grated (about ¾ cup)

⅓ cup raisins

2 tablespoons mayonnaise

½ teaspoon curry powder (optional)

4 (4-inch) whole-wheat pita bread pockets

4 lettuce leaves

In Batter Bowl, flake tuna with Pastry Blender. Add carrot, raisins, mayonnaise and curry powder and mix well.

Cut about 1 inch from the side of each pita round and gently separate insides to form a pocket. Line each pita pocket with a lettuce leaf, then spoon in a quarter of the Tuna-Carrot Salad mixture. Repeat for additional sandwiches.

Yield: 4 sandwiches

TURKEY-APPLE SALAD SANDWICHES

⅓ cup chopped cooked turkey

2 tablespoons chopped apple

2 tablespoons chopped celery

2 tablespoons mayonnaise

16 slices white or whole-wheat bread

Using Food Chopper, chop and measure turkey, apple and celery; turn into Batter Bowl. Add mayonnaise and mix well.

Place 1 scant tablespoon turkey-apple salad in center of bread slice and top with second bread slice. Use the 3-inch Cut-N-Seal to cut and seal round sandwich. Repeat for additional sandwiches.

Yield: 8 sandwiches

Autumn Apple Fest

Crunching leaves. Early dusk. Sweater weather. And apples, of course. The orchards are heavy with fruit just begging to be baked into old-time desserts: cinnamon-and-spice and cheddary treats that will make your house smell good for days. Whether you pick your own apples or buy them by the bushel at a roadside market, you'll no doubt have plenty to share with family and friends. So invite a bunch over for a lively game of touch football. Better yet, hand them some leaf rakes — and thank them for their hard work with a cozy Autumn Apple Fest.

SPICED APPLE STIR-FRY

▪

VANILLA ICE CREAM OR
FROZEN YOGURT

▪

CARAMEL APPLE DIP

▪

CHEDDAR-APPLE
DESSERT PIZZA

▪

CRANBERRY-APPLE CRISP

▪

HOT MULLED CIDER

SPICED APPLE STIR-FRY

3 medium Granny Smith
  apples

1 teaspoon grated fresh ginger

⅓ cup sugar

¼ teaspoon ground cinnamon

⅛ teaspoon ground allspice

⅛ teaspoon ground nutmeg

⅛ teaspoon ground cloves

⅓ cup apple cider or juice

1 teaspoon cornstarch

2 tablespoons butter or
  margarine

Peel, core and slice apples with Apple Peeler/Corer/Slicer. Cut stacked apple slices into fourths and set aside. In small bowl, mix together the sugar, cinnamon, allspice, nutmeg and cloves; set aside. In a separate bowl, whisk cider with cornstarch; set aside.

In Stir-Fry Skillet over medium heat, melt butter. Add apples and grated ginger and stir-fry for 2 minutes. Stir in sugar-spice mixture and stir-fry for an additional 2 minutes. Stir in cider-cornstarch mixture and cook, stirring constantly, until it comes to a boil and is slightly thickened. Serve warm over vanilla ice cream or frozen yogurt.

Yield: 4 to 5 servings

CARAMEL APPLE DIP

1 package (8 ounces) cream
  cheese, softened

⅓ cup apple butter*

¼ cup brown sugar, packed

⅓ teaspoon vanilla extract

⅓ cup peanuts, chopped

Apples, quartered, for dipping

In Batter Bowl mix cream cheese, apple butter, brown sugar and vanilla with Bamboo Spoon until smooth. Chop peanuts with Food Chopper and stir into cream cheese mixture. Cover and chill several hours or overnight.

Just before serving, peel apples. Using Apple Wedger, core and cut into wedges. Arrange apple quarters around bowl filled with Caramel Apple Dip and serve.

Yield: About 2 cups dip

Variation: Substitute 1 can (8 ounces) crushed pineapple, drained, in place of apple butter.

* Look for apple butter in the jam and jelly section of your supermarket.

Crust:

1 ¼ cups all-purpose flour

1 teaspoon salt

½ cup vegetable shortening

1 cup shredded Cheddar cheese

¼ cup ice water

Topping:

½ cup brown sugar, packed

½ cup sugar

⅓ cup all-purpose flour

1 teaspoon ground cinnamon

½ teaspoon ground nutmeg

¼ teaspoon salt

*¼ cup butter or margarine,
    softened*

4 medium apples

2 tablespoons lemon juice

CHEDDAR-APPLE DESSERT PIZZA

Preheat oven to 375° F. Prepare crust: In Batter Bowl, combine flour with salt. With Pastry Blender, cut in shortening until crumbly. Add cheese and toss lightly. Sprinkle ice water gradually over mixture, then shape into a ball with lightly floured hands. Place dough in center of the 13-inch Round Baking Stone and with Dough and Pizza Roller, roll outward from center in all directions to cover Baking Stone. Pinch edges of dough upward to form a 1-inch rim.

Prepare topping: In bowl, mix sugars with flour, cinnamon, nutmeg and salt. Spinkle half of sugar mixture over crust. Cut butter into remaining sugar mixture until crumbly and set aside. Peel, core and slice apples using Apple Peeler/Corer/Slicer. Arrange apple rings on crust in overlapping circles. Sprinkle with lemon juice, then with sugar-butter mixture. Bake 35 to 40 minutes, or until apples are tender and crust is browned around edges. Serve warm.

Yield: 12 servings

Making the Dessert Pizza

1. With Dough and Pizza Roller, roll pastry outward from center of Baking Stone to cover. Pinch edges upward to form 1-inch rim.

2. Peel, core and slice apples using Apple Peeler/Corer/Slicer. Arrange spiral apple slices evenly over crumb-topped crust.

3. Sprinkle apple slices with lemon juice, then with remaining topping.

Filling:

5 medium Granny Smith apples

*1 can (16 ounces) whole-berry
    cranberry sauce*

¾ cup sugar

2 tablespoons all-purpose flour

Topping:

¼ cup walnuts, chopped

1 cup rolled oats

⅓ cup brown sugar, packed

⅓ cup all-purpose flour

1 teaspoon ground cinnamon

*¼ cup butter or margarine,
    melted*

CRANBERRY-APPLE CRISP

Preheat oven to 375° F. Prepare filling: Peel, core and slice apples with Apple Peeler/Corer/Slicer. Cut stack of apple slices in half and place slices in 9"x 13" Baker. In Batter Bowl, mix cranberry sauce with sugar and flour, then toss mixture with apple slices in Baker.

Prepare topping: Chop walnuts finely with Food Chopper. In Batter Bowl, mix walnuts with oats, brown sugar, flour and cinnamon. Mix in melted butter, then sprinkle topping evenly over apple-cranberry mixture. Bake 30 to 40 minutes, or until topping is golden brown and fruit is tender.

Yield: 15 servings

Good Report Card

When the news from school is good, everyone's happy: you, the teacher and especially the star pupil. Show your child how proud you are by preparing a fun meal with lively Southwestern fare that can't help but make everyone grin. The evening will seem even more special with a few simple decorations tied into the spirit of the event: a bunch of colorful balloons, perhaps, or a big, bright-yellow construction-paper star to serve as a placemat for the guest of honor. It all adds up to a great big pat on the back for a student who's working hard to succeed — and you can't ask much more than that.

FIESTA CHILI
CORN BREAD

◾

GAZPACHO
SALAD

◾

BANANA SPLIT

◾

MILK

Crust:

2 packages (8 ½ ounces each)
   corn-muffin mix

2 eggs, lightly beaten

⅔ cup milk

1 can (11 ounces) Mexican-style
   corn, drained*

Filling:

1 can (15 ounces) no-beans chili

1 cup shredded Cheddar cheese

1 cup shredded Monterey Jack
   cheese

½ cup chopped scallions,
   including tops

1 can (2 ¼ ounces) chopped
   black olives

Sour cream for garnish
   (optional)

FIESTA CHILI CORN BREAD

Preheat oven to 350° F. Prepare crusts: Lightly spray 2 Flan Pans with non-stick vegetable spray. In Batter Bowl combine corn-muffin mix, eggs, milk and corn; stir to combine. Pour half of batter into each Flan Pan and bake 20 minutes. Cool corn-bread crusts in pans 10 minutes, then turn out and arrange on serving trays.

Prepare filling: Meanwhile, in 1½-quart Generation II Saucepan, heat chili over medium heat. Spread half of hot chili evenly in the well of each corn-bread crust. Evenly distribute cheeses, scallions, and olives over chili and garnish with sour cream, if desired. Cut into wedges with Pizza Cutter and serve with Mini-Serving Spatula.

Yield: 2 corn-bread rounds (6 to 8 servings each)

* Corn with red and green peppers

3 medium tomatoes, coarsely
    chopped

1 ½ medium green peppers,
    coarsely chopped

1 medium cucumber, coarsely
    chopped

⅓ cup diced red onion

2 to 3 garlic cloves, pressed

2 tablespoons olive oil

2 teaspoons red wine vinegar

Salt and ground black pepper
    to taste

GAZPACHO SALAD

Combine tomatoes, green pepper, cucumber and red onion in Batter Bowl. In small bowl, whisk together garlic, olive oil and vinegar using 10-inch Whisk. Pour dressing over vegetables; stir to combine with Super Scraper. Season with salt and pepper.

Yield: 6 to 8 servings

Pumpkin Carving

The Halloween fun begins with trying to figure out just what kind of character your pumpkin should become: Scary? Happy? Silly? The Pumpkin Cutter will help you give it the personality it deserves. Get the Chunky Beef Chili going before you start, and then let the kids draw faces on their own smaller pumpkins as you carve out the family jack-o'-lantern. The chili will be ready about the same time as the pumpkin, so wedge a candle in the bottom and dine by the flickering glow of your spooky new centerpiece!

CHUNKY BEEF CHILI

■

PIZZA BREAD STICKS

■

CANDY APPLE
DELIGHT

■

LEMONADE OR
ORANGEADE

2 large onions, chopped

2 celery stalks, chopped

2 garlic cloves, pressed

2 tablespoons vegetable oil

2 pounds beef chuck, cut in ½-inch cubes

1 tablespoon ground cumin

1 tablespoon dried oregano

1 tablespoon chili powder

½ teaspoon salt

¼ teaspoon cayenne pepper

¼ teaspoon ground black pepper

1 can (28 ounces) whole tomatoes, with juice

2 cups water

CHUNKY BEEF CHILI

With Food Chopper, chop onions and celery. Press garlic with Garlic Press; set aside. Heat 1 tablespoon of oil in 6-quart Generation II Dutch Oven over medium-high heat. Add half of beef cubes and cook, stirring occasionally with Bamboo Spoon, until browned on all sides, about 8 minutes. Remove browned beef from Dutch oven and set aside. Repeat browning process with remaining oil and beef, and remove beef after browning.

Add onions, celery and garlic to drippings in Dutch oven and cook over low heat 5 minutes, stirring frequently. Return browned beef to Dutch oven. Stir in cumin, oregano, chili powder, salt, cayenne and black pepper. With Kitchen Cutters, cut tomatoes into chunks. Add tomatoes with their juice and the water to beef mixture. Bring chili to a simmer and cook, uncovered, over low heat until meat is very tender — 2 to 3 hours. Add more water, 1/2 cup at a time, if necessary to reach desired consistency.

Yield: 8 servings

1 loaf (16 ounces) frozen bread dough, thawed

3 tablespoons olive oil

1 to 2 garlic cloves, pressed

⅓ cup grated Parmesan cheese

½ cup shredded mozzarella cheese

1 can (8 ounces) pizza sauce

PIZZA BREAD STICKS

Preheat oven to 400° F. Fold dough, press out bubbles and knead until elastic and smooth. Stretch and pat dough onto 12" x 15" Rectangle Baking Stone, stretching dough over sides. (Dough may resist stretching but will eventually relax.) Cover dough with dampened towel and let rest in a warm spot for 15 minutes.

Brush dough evenly with olive oil. Press garlic through Garlic Press and spread evenly over oiled dough. Grate Parmesan cheese with Cheese Grater; sprinkle Parmesan and mozzarella evenly over dough. Bake 12 to 15 minutes or until light golden brown. Cut into long strips with Pizza Cutter and serve with pizza sauce for dipping.

Yield: Varies according to size of breadsticks

1 container (8 ounces) frozen whipped topping, thawed

2 cans (8 ounces each) crushed pineapple, drained

3 Granny Smith apples

3 Snickers candy bars, 2.07 ounces each

½ cup peanuts

CANDY APPLE DELIGHT

Combine whipped topping and pineapple in Batter Bowl. Peel, core and slice apples with Apple Peeler/Corer/Slicer, then cut slices into quarters. With Garnisher, cut candy bars into small cubes. With Food Chopper, chop peanuts. Fold apples, candy and peanuts into whipped topping mixture. Serve immediately or refrigerate, covered, for 1 to 2 hours.

Yield: About 7 cups

Dinner for Six

Few things are as satisfying as a good meal, with good friends, in the casual comfort of your own dining room. With no one rushing you out, and with five of your favorite people gathered around, you can truly relax and enjoy conversation that goes much deeper than cocktail chatter ever could. Classic Chicken Cacciatore with fettuccine, followed by a heady Almond Cheesecake, is certainly a meal to linger over. Go ahead — help yourself to seconds. No one's waiting for your table!

CHICKEN
CACCIATORE

▪

FETTUCCINE

▪

TOSSED SALAD

▪

DILL MIX SALAD
DRESSING

▪

ROLLS

▪

ALMOND
CHEESECAKE WITH
CHOCOLATE-ALMOND
CRUST

Chicken Cacciatore

1 broiler/fryer chicken (about 3 pounds), cut in serving pieces

1 tablespoon olive oil

6 scallions, sliced diagonally in 1-inch pieces

1 large green pepper, cut in ½-inch strips

2 garlic cloves, pressed

½ teaspoon dried oregano

½ teaspoon salt

¼ teaspoon ground black pepper

1 can (6 ounces) tomato paste

½ cup dry white wine

10 pitted black olives, coarsely chopped

8 ounces fresh mushrooms, thinly sliced

Wash chicken pieces, dry with paper towels and trim off excess fat. Brush Stir-Fry Skillet with olive oil and set over medium heat. When Stir-Fry Skillet is hot, add chicken and brown on all sides, turning as necessary. Push chicken to one side of skillet and add scallions, green pepper, garlic, oregano, salt and pepper. Cook, stirring occasionally, for 10 minutes or until vegetables begin to color.

Meanwhile, in small bowl, mix tomato paste with wine and olives. Stir into chicken and vegetables, cover with Stir-Fry Skillet Lid, and cook over low heat about 30 minutes, or until juices run clear when chicken breast or thigh is pierced in thickest part. Add mushrooms, cover and cook 10 minutes longer.

Yield: 6 servings

Dill Mix Salad Dressing

1 cup mayonnaise

1 cup sour cream

6 to 7 tablespoons milk

3 tablespoons All-Purpose Dill Mix

Combine mayonnaise, sour cream, milk and Dill Mix in mixing bowl. With Mini-Whipper, beat until smooth and well blended. Cover and refrigerate at least 1 hour before serving.

Yield: about 2 cups

Crust:

¼ cup butter or margarine

1 square (1 ounce) semisweet chocolate, cut into pieces

½ cup blanched almonds, finely chopped

1 ¼ cups graham cracker crumbs (about 15 crackers)

Filling:

2 cups (16 ounces) ricotta cheese

1 package (8 ounces) cream cheese, softened

1 can (8 ounces) almond paste

¼ cup sugar

3 eggs

1 teaspoon vanilla extract

ALMOND CHEESECAKE WITH CHOCOLATE-ALMOND CRUST

Preheat oven to 375° F. Prepare crust: Melt butter and chocolate over low heat in 1½-quart Generation II Saucepan. With Food Chopper, finely chop almonds. In Batter Bowl, mix melted butter and chocolate with almonds and graham cracker crumbs until well blended. Press chocolate-crumb mixture over bottom and halfway up sides of Springform Pan fitted with flat bottom; set aside.

Prepare filling: In mixer bowl, beat ricotta, cream cheese and almond paste until smooth and creamy. Beat in sugar and then eggs, one at a time, beating well after each addition. Beat in vanilla. Carefully pour filling into crust. Bake 1 hour or until filling is set and golden around edges. Cool in pan on Non-Stick Cooling Rack, then cover with plastic wrap and refrigerate several hours or overnight.

To serve, run knife around sides of pan to loosen cheesecake. Then set Springform Pan on a serving plate and remove collar, leaving cheesecake on flat pan bottom. Garnish with rosettes of whipped cream and chocolate-dipped blanched almonds.

Yield: 10 to 12 servings

School Party Treats

Being a Mom means being asked to bake: for Scout meetings and Sunday school, for birthday parties and bake sales. Next time you're on duty, go for something delightfully different: Chocolate-dipped pretzels. Crispy cereal baskets with licorice-whip "handles." A cookie pizza. Or the old standby, cupcakes, with surprising new twists on top and inside. You'll shoot right to the top of everyone's baking list — but since these are so easy, you won't mind being called again and again.

MINI-BASKET CRISPY TREATS

¼ cup butter or margarine

1 package (10 ounces) mini
  marshmallows

5 ½ cups crisp rice cereal

48 2-inch pieces red licorice
  whip

192 (about 8 ounces) small
  jelly beans

In 2-quart Generation II Saucepan, melt butter over low heat. Add marshmallows and stir until marshmallows are melted and mixture is smooth, about 2 minutes. Remove from heat, stir in cereal. Working quickly, spoon mixture into cups of 4 Mini-Muffin Pans. Dip Mini-Tart Shaper into water and press into each cup to form a basket, dipping shaper into water as necessary to prevent sticking. Press licorice whip into sides of each basket to form handle. Let baskets cool 30 minutes, then remove from pans and fill with jelly beans.

Yield: 4 dozen mini-baskets

DIPPED PRETZEL RODS

1 package (12 ounces) semisweet chocolate chips

30 pretzel rods, about 11 ounces

Toppings:

  Finely chopped peanuts

  Candy sprinkles

  Shredded coconut

Cover baking sheet with wax paper. Melt chocolate in Batter Bowl according to package directions. Dip one end of each pretzel in melted chocolate, then roll in desired topping. Arrange on wax paper-covered baking sheet and refrigerate until chocolate is set.

Yield: 30 rods

CAT CUPCAKES

1 box (18 to 19 ounces) cake mix, any flavor

3 cups chocolate icing

210 (about 9 ounces) small jelly beans

60 3-inch pieces black licorice whip

Preheat oven to 350° F. Spray 5 Mini-Muffin Pans with non-stick vegetable spray. Prepare cake batter according to package directions; spoon into prepared Mini-Muffin Pans, filling cups 2/3 full with batter. Bake 15 minutes or until Cake Tester inserted in center of a cupcake comes out clean. Cool cupcakes in pans 15 minutes, then turn onto cooling rack to finish cooling.

Spread each cupcake with icing using Icing Spreader. Use 2 jelly beans to makes ears for each cat; cut remaining jelly beans in half to make eyes and noses. Cut each licorice piece into six 1/2-inch lengths to make whiskers.

Yield: 5 dozen mini cupcakes

SURPRISE CUPCAKES

1 box (18 to 19 ounces) cake mix, any flavor

2 cups icing, any flavor

Surprise Options:
  Candy-coated chocolate pieces

  Gumdrops

  Chocolate kisses

  Jelly beans

Preheat oven to 350° F. Spray 5 Mini-Muffin Pans with non-stick vegetable spray. Prepare cake batter according to package directions; spoon into prepared Mini-Muffin Pans, filling cups 2/3 full with batter. Bake 8 minutes, remove from oven, and top each cupcake with a surprise. Return to oven and bake another 3 to 4 minutes. Cool cupcakes in pans 15 minutes, then remove from pans to finish cooling. Use Decorating Set to cover each cupcake with a swirl of icing, then top each one with an additional surprise.

Yield: 5 dozen mini cupcakes

RAINY DAY CUPCAKES

1 box (18 to 19 ounces) cake mix, any flavor

2 cups icing

60 small paper umbrellas

60 (about 9 ounces) small gumdrops

Preheat oven to 350° F. Spray 5 Mini-Muffin Pans with non-stick vegetable spray. Prepare cake batter according to package directions; spoon into prepared Mini-Muffin Pans, filling cups 2/3 full with batter. Bake 15 minutes or until Cake Tester inserted in center of a cupcake comes out clean. Cool cupcakes in pans 15 minutes, then turn onto cooling rack to finish cooling. Use Decorating Set to frost tops of cupcakes. Stick handle of each umbrella into a gumdrop and press gently into icing on top of cupcake.

Yield: 5 dozen mini cupcakes

COOKIE PIZZA

1 package (20 ounces) refrigerated sugar-cookie dough

1 cup vanilla icing

1 cup shredded coconut, toasted

15 large red gumdrops, flattened slightly

8 medium-size green gumdrops, cut in half

⅓ cup chopped black licorice whip

3 tablespoons chopped pecans

Preheat oven to 350° F. With lightly floured Dough and Pizza Roller, roll cookie dough into 14-inch circle on 15-inch Round Baking Stone. Bake 15 minutes or until lightly browned. While still warm, cut into 12 wedges with Pizza Cutter and press wedges back into place to form a tight circle. Cool completely, then spread evenly with icing. Sprinkle with coconut to resemble cheese, arrange red and green gumdrops over coconut for "pepperoni" and "peppers," and sprinkle with chopped licorice and pecans.

Yield: 12 cookie wedges

Sunday Dinner

Here's to an old-fashioned tradition that never really went out of style. Rediscover the joy of a simple and slow-paced Sunday dinner with the family, and you'll remember why you loved it so much in your youth. It gives you the chance to take a break from the hustle and bustle of the week (and maybe even the weekend) and relax with everyone gathered around. Watch a ball game on television or maybe do a crossword puzzle together while the comforting aroma of an herb-roasted chicken fills the house and envelops you in all its homey warmth. Eat a bit earlier than usual and the evening will seem that much longer — a nice way to gear up for the week ahead.

EASY OVEN-ROASTED
CHICKEN

■

POTATOES ANNA

■

BUTTERED GREEN
BEANS

■

ROLLS

■

BANANA CREAM
SUPREME

1 broiler/fryer chicken (2 ½ to 3 pounds)

1 teaspoon Italian herb mix

Salt and ground black pepper to taste

EASY OVEN-ROASTED CHICKEN

Preheat oven to 350° F. Rinse chicken and pat dry with paper towels. Sprinkle with herb mix, salt and pepper. Place in Deep Dish Baker, breast side up. Cover with Baking Bowl and roast 1 hour 15 minutes, or until juices run clear when thickest part of thigh is pierced. During the last 15 to 20 minutes of roasting, remove Baking Bowl so chicken will brown.

Yield: 3 to 4 servings

6 large baking potatoes (about 4 pounds)

½ cup butter or margarine, melted

Salt and ground black pepper

POTATOES ANNA

Preheat oven to 425° F. With Vegetable Peeler, peel potatoes, then slice thinly with Vario-Slicer. Brush bottom and sides of Mini Baking Bowl generously with butter. Arrange single, slightly overlapping layer of potato slices in bottom of bowl; brush with butter, and sprinkle with salt and pepper. Continue layering potatoes with butter, salt and pepper until bowl is filled to the brim. Pour any remaining butter over potatoes, cover with inverted 8-inch Mini Baker and bake 15 minutes. Reduce oven temperature to 350° F and bake additional 1 hour 15 minutes, or until potatoes are tender. Remove Mini Baker and bake another 10 to 15 minutes, or until potatoes are crisp and golden. Let stand on cooling rack 5 minutes, then carefully run metal spatula around edges of bowl and invert potatoes onto serving plate, if desired. Serve hot.

Yield: 6 servings

24 graham cracker squares
(2 ½ inches each)

½ cup butter or margarine,
melted

¼ cup sugar

1 container (12 ounces) frozen
whipped topping, thawed

1 package (3.4 ounces) instant
vanilla pudding mix

1 cup sour cream

3 medium bananas

⅓ cup chopped pecans

BANANA CREAM SUPREME

With Food Chopper, finely chop graham crackers; you should have about 2 cups crumbs. In medium bowl, mix graham cracker crumbs with butter and sugar; press evenly over bottom and two-thirds of the way up sides of Springform Pan.

In Batter Bowl, combine whipped topping, pudding mix and sour cream; stir vigorously with 10-inch Whisk. Spread half of filling into crust. With Egg Slicer, slice bananas and layer evenly over filling in pan. Spread remaining filling over bananas. In Food Chopper, finely chop pecans, then sprinkle over top of filling.

Note: Filling sets quickly, but should be refrigerated at least 30 minutes before serving, to be at desirable serving temperature.

Yield: 12 servings

Christmas-Cookie Baking Fun

Christmas is a time of sharing, from our hands and our hearts, and some leisurely afternoon cookie-baking with the kids gives you the chance to do a little of both. While homemade cookies make wonderful, well-appreciated gifts, the luckiest people are not the ones getting the treats, but the ones giving them, because with all the mixing and rolling and decorating, they've shared the most important gift of all: their time. Children and adults alike will love creating colorful Jam Thumbprints, rich Pecan Balls and festive Twinkling Gingerbread Stars, made simpler with packaged mix and a surprise ingredient for the "stained glass" center. Savor the aroma of cookies baking and enjoy a glass of Cranberry Punch when you're all done.

JAM THUMBPRINTS

▪

PECAN BALLS

▪

TWINKLING
GINGERBREAD STARS

▪

CRANBERRY PUNCH

2 cups fresh strawberries or frozen strawberries partially thawed, chopped

4 cups chilled cranberry juice

2 tablespoons lemon juice

2 cups chilled ginger ale

Whole strawberries for garnish (optional)

CRANBERRY PUNCH

Chop strawberries with Food Chopper. In Batter Bowl, combine strawberries, cranberry juice and lemon juice; stir well. Just before serving, add ginger ale. Ladle into punch cups or glasses and garnish each serving with a whole strawberry, if desired. *Yield: 8 cups*

½ cup butter or margarine,
softened

⅓ cup sugar

1 egg yolk

1 teaspoon vanilla extract

1 ⅓ cups all-purpose flour

¼ cup jam, jelly or marmalade,
any flavor

⅓ cup slivered blanched
almonds

JAM THUMBPRINTS

Preheat oven to 350° F. In mixer bowl, cream butter on high speed until light and fluffy. Add sugar and continue beating until well blended; beat in egg yolk and vanilla. On low speed, gradually add flour until completely blended. (Dough will be quite firm.)

Using small Stainless Steel Scoop, drop cookies 2 inches apart onto 15-inch Round Baking Stone. With rounded side of scoop, make a deep indentation in center of each cookie. Bake 8 to 10 minutes or until cookies are firm but not brown.

Remove Baking Stone from oven and fill center of each cookie with 1/2 teaspoon of jam. Sprinkle jam centers with slivered almonds. Return cookies to oven and bake 8 to 12 minutes longer, or until lightly browned. Cool cookies on stone 2 to 3 minutes, then transfer to Non-Stick Cooling Rack to finish cooling.

Yield: about 2 dozen cookies

1 ½ cups pecans, finely
chopped

1 cup butter or margarine,
softened

½ cup sugar

2 teaspoons vanilla extract

2 cups all-purpose flour

Confectioners' sugar

PECAN BALLS

Preheat oven to 300° F. Finely chop pecans with Food Chopper; set aside. Combine butter and sugar in mixer bowl and beat on medium speed until light and fluffy. Beat in vanilla extract. On low speed, blend in flour and pecans until well blended.

With small Stainless Steel Scoop, drop cookies 1 inch apart onto 15-inch Round Baking Stone. Bake 18 to 20 minutes or until cookies just begin to brown around edges. Cool 2 to 3 minutes on stone, then transfer to Non-Stick Cooling Rack to finish cooling. Sprinkle with confectioners' sugar while still warm.

Yield: about 3 ½ dozen cookies

1 box (14 ½ ounces) gingerbread cake and cookie mix

2 tablespoons flour

2 packages Lifesaver candies,
   mixed fruit flavors

TWINKLING GINGERBREAD STARS

Preheat oven to 375º F. Prepare gingerbread mix according to package directions for cookies. Divide and shape dough into two balls.

With Dough and Pizza Roller dusted with enough flour to prevent sticking, roll dough 1/8-inch thick onto 18" x 12" Cutting Board. Using Star-Shaped Valtrompia Bread Tube, cut dough into star shapes. Carefully transfer star shapes onto 12" x 15" Rectangle Baking Stone.

With Apple Corer, cut out a circle of dough from the center of each cookie and carefully remove; place a Lifesaver candy in each center. Bake 10 minutes. (Candies will melt and give stained glass effect.) Cool cookies on Baking Stone 5 minutes, then remove to rack to finish cooling.

Yield: about 24 cookies

Making the Gingerbread Stars

1. Roll dough about ⅛-inch thick with Dough and Pizza Roller. Cut into star shapes with Valtrompia Bread Tube and arrange on Rectangle Baking Stone.

2. With Apple Corer, cut a circle from center of each cookie, then fill with a candy before baking.

Christmas Eve Caroling Party

The cards are mailed, the last present wrapped, and now there's nothing to do but relax and reflect on the true meaning of the holiday. Why not start a new Christmas Eve tradition with an old-fashioned caroling party for your family and friends? Provide a festive atmosphere of twinkling lights, a roaring fire, and a buffet table laden with special food that radiates the warmth of the evening. Since you've made it all ahead, you can spend your time with the chorale, not in the kitchen — a lovely respite from the hubbub of the season and the busy day tomorrow.

VERMONT CHEDDAR
SPREAD
▪
CANAPÉ BREAD
▪
HOLIDAY WRAPPINGS
▪
SAUCY MEATBALLS
▪
FRUIT SKEWERS WITH
RASPBERRY DIP
▪
MERRY CHRISTMOUSSE
▪
HOT CHOCOLATE

1 package (3 ounces) cream
   cheese, softened

¼ cup butter, softened

2 cups coarsely grated sharp
   white Cheddar cheese

3 tablespoons chopped fresh
   chives

½ teaspoon dry mustard

Pinch cayenne pepper

VERMONT CHEDDAR SPREAD

In Batter Bowl with electric mixer, beat cream cheese and butter until well blended. Add Cheddar cheese, chives, mustard and cayenne, and beat until well blended and fluffy. Transfer Cheddar spread to serving bowl, cover and refrigerate. Serve with star-shaped Valtrompia canapé bread slices.

Yield: 1 ¾ cups

---

1 package (10 ounces)
   refrigerated bread dough

CANAPÉ BREAD

Preheat oven to 400° F. Spray inside of Valtrompia Bread Tube with non-stick vegetable spray. Bake bread 50 to 60 minutes in tube. Cool. Slice bread into thin slices.

Yield: 28 to 32 slices

*2 packages (3 ounces each)
  cream cheese, softened*

½ cup sour cream

1 garlic clove, pressed

¾ teaspoon All-Purpose Dill Mix

⅛ teaspoon ground black pepper

*1 package (2 ½ ounces)
  processed sliced beef*

½ cup shredded Swiss cheese

*2 tablespoons shredded
  Parmesan cheese*

36 wonton wrappers

HOLIDAY WRAPPINGS

Preheat oven to 350° F. In Batter Bowl, blend cream cheese until smooth with sour cream, garlic, Dill Mix and pepper. With Food Chopper, chop beef finely in batches and add to cream cheese mixture, along with Swiss and Parmesan cheeses; blend well.

Spray 3 Mini-Muffin Pans with non-stick vegetable spray. Separate wonton wrappers and arrange one in each cup of the Mini-Muffin Pans. With Mini-Tart Shaper, press each wonton wrapper into muffin cup. With small Stainless Steel Scoop, fill wonton cups with cheese mixture. Dip fingers in cold water, then pinch and twist tops of each wonton together to form package. Bake 15 minutes or until wontons are browned and crisp. Cool 10 minutes before serving. Serve warm.

Yield: 36 hors d'oeuvres

Making the Holiday Wrappings

1. In Batter Bowl, using Super Scraper, blend cream cheese with sour cream and seasonings until smooth.

2. With Mini-Tart Shaper, press wonton wrappers into cup shapes in Mini-Muffin Pan. Fill with beef-cheese mixture, using small Stainless Steel Scoop.

3. Dip fingers in water and pinch tops of each wonton wrapper together to form bundle.

Meatballs:

2 pounds lean ground beef

3 eggs, slightly beaten

1 cup dry bread crumbs

1 package (1 ½ ounces) dry onion soup mix

Sauce:

1 can (16 ounces) whole-berry cranberry sauce

1 bottle (12 ounces) chili sauce

1 cup light brown sugar, packed

1 can (14 ounces) sauerkraut, rinsed and drained

1 cup water

SAUCY MEATBALLS

Preheat oven to 350° F. Prepare meatballs: In large bowl, combine ground beef, eggs, bread crumbs and onion soup mix until well blended. With small Stainless Steel Scoop, shape meatballs and arrange in single layer in 9" x 13" Baker.

Prepare sauce: In Batter Bowl, combine cranberry sauce, chili sauce, brown sugar, sauerkraut and water. Stir with 10-inch Whisk until well blended, then pour evenly over meatballs. Bake 50 to 55 minutes or until meatballs are done.

Yield: about 7 dozen meatballs

½ cup cream cheese, softened

½ cup vanilla yogurt

¼ cup fresh or frozen unsweetened raspberries

2 teaspoons confectioners' sugar

Fresh fruits, such as strawberries, cantaloupe, pineapple, grapes, kiwi, peaches, bananas, apples

FRUIT SKEWERS WITH RASPBERRY DIP

In Batter Bowl, combine cream cheese, yogurt, raspberries and confectioners' sugar; cream with Bamboo Spoon until smooth. Chill. Prepare fruit by washing, coring, stemming and peeling as necessary. Cut larger fruits into chunks using 5-inch Self-Sharpening Utility Knife.

Thread fruit onto skewers, arrange around dip and serve.

Yield: 1 cup

½ cup cold water

2 envelopes unflavored gelatin

1 package (3 ounces, 24 count) ladyfingers

2 packages (3.9 ounces each) instant chocolate pudding mix

3 cups milk

1 container (8 ounces) frozen whipped topping, thawed

6 round peppermint candies

Mint sprigs

Whole cranberries

MERRY CHRISTMOUSSE

Add water to Microwave Saucepan, sprinkle with gelatin and stir to blend. Set aside 2 minutes to soften. Then microwave on 100 percent power for 40 seconds to 1 minute, or until gelatin is dissolved. Stir well and set aside to cool 5 minutes.

Meanwhile, cut ladyfingers in half lengthwise and crumble 24 halves into Springform Pan fitted with flat bottom. With hands palm down, press the crumbled ladyfingers evenly over base. Arrange remaining 24 ladyfinger halves upright, rounded sides out, around inner collar of pan; set aside.

In Batter Bowl, combine pudding mix, milk and softened gelatin. Whisk with 10-inch Whisk until smooth and well blended. Fold in whipped topping. Spoon mousse into ladyfinger-lined Springform Pan, cover loosely with plastic wrap and refrigerate until firm, at least 30 minutes.

To serve, set mousse on serving plate, then release and remove collar of Springform Pan. Chop peppermint candies finely with Food Chopper and sprinkle over mousse. Arrange mint sprigs and cranberries around mousse to resemble holly.

Yield: 12 to 15 servings

Variation: Substitute 25 vanilla wafers for ladyfingers, crushing 10 cookies for base and arranging 15 around inner collar of Springform Pan.